The Song Celestial
Or
Bhagavad-Gita

Translated by

Sir Edwin Arnold

ISBN: 978-1-63923-538-4

Printed: October 2022

Cover Art By: Amit Paul

Published and Distributed By:
Lushena Books
607 Country Club Drive, Unit E
Bensenville, IL 60106
www.lushenabks.com

ISBN: 978-1-63923-538-4

So have I read this wonderful and spirit-thrilling speech,

By Krishna and Prince Arjun heJd, discoursing each with each;

So have I writ its wisdom here, its hidden mystery.

For England; O our India/ as dear to me as She!

Edwin Arnold

PREFACE

This famous and marvelous Sanskrit poem occurs as an episode of the Maha-bharata, in the sixth—or "Bishma" —Parva of the great Hindu epic. It enjoys immense popularity and authority in India, where it is reckoned as one of the 'Tive Jewels"— pancharatnani—of Devanagari literature. In plain but noble language it unfolds a philosophical system which remains to this day the prevailing Brahmanic belief, blending as it does with the doctrines of Ka-pila, Patanjali, and the Vedas. So lofty are many of its declarations, so sublime its aspirations, so pure and tender its piety, that Schlegel, after his study of the poem, breaks forth into this outburst of delight and praise towards its unknown author: "Magistorum reverentia a Brachmanis inter sanctissima pietatis officia refertur. Ergo te primum, Vates sanctissime, Numinisque hypophetal quisquis tandem inter mortaJes

dictus tu fueris, carminis jujus auctor, cu-jus oracuJis mens ad excelsa quaeque aeter-na atque divina, cum inenarrabiJi quadam deJectatione rapitur—te primum, inquam, salvere juheo, et vestigia tua semper adoro." * Lassen re-echoes this splendid tribute; and indeed, so striking are some of the moralities here inculcated, and so close the parallelism—ofttimes actually verbal—between its teachings and those of the New Testament, that a controversy has arisen between Pandits and Missionaries on the point whether the author borrowed from Christian sources, or the Evangelists and

Apostles from him. This raises the question of its date, which cannot be positively settled. It must have been inlaid into the ancient epic at a period other than that of the original Maha-bharata, but Mr. Kasinath Telang has offered

* "Among the holiest observances of piety noted down by the Brahmins is reverence toward the masters. I wish, therefore, to salute thee first, most holy prophet and interpreter of the Divinity, whosoever thou hast been said to be among mortals, author of that poem the prophetic sayings of which carry the mind with certain unerring delight to all that is lofty, eternal, and divine— and I worship forever thy footsteps." (Publisher's Note)

PREFACE [ix]

some fair argument to prove it anterior to the Christian era. The weight of evidence, howrever, tends to place its composition at about the third century after Christ; and perhaps there are really echoes in this Brah-manic poem of the lesson of Galilee, and of the Sjrrian incarnation.*

Its scene is the level country betv^een the Jumna and the Sarsooti rivers— nov^ Kurnal and Jheend. Its simple plot consists of a dialogue held by Prince Arjuna, the brother of King Yudhisthira, with Krishna, the Supreme Deity, wearing the disguise of a charioteer. A great battle is impending between the armies of the Kauravas and Pandavas, and this conversation is maintained in a war chariot drawn up between the opposing hosts.

The poem has been turned into French by Burnouf, into Latin by Lassen, into Italian by Stanislav Gatti, into Greek by Galan-os, and into English by Mr. Thomson and

* Although this was the belief of scholars in the late nineteenth century, scholars nowadays generally agree that its origin precedes by several centuries the Christian era. (Pubiisher's Note)

Mr. Davies, the prose transcript of the last-named being truly beyond praise for its fidelity and clearness. Mr. Telang has also published at Bombay a version in colloquial rhythm, eminently learned and intelligent, but not conveying the dignity or grace of the original. If I venture to offer a translation of the wonderful poem after so many superior scholars, it is in grateful recognition of the help derived from their labors and because English literature would certainly be incomplete without possessing in popular form a poetical and philosophical work so dear to India.

There is little else to say which the Song Celestial does not explain for itself. The Sanskrit original is written in the Anushtubh meter, which cannot be successfully reproduced for Western ears. I have therefore cast it into our flexible blank verse, changing into lyrical measures where the text itself similarly breaks. For the most part, I believe the sense to be faithfully preserved in the following pages; but Schlegel himself had to say: "In reconditioribus me semper poetae mentem

rede divinasse affirmare non ausim."* Those who would read more upon the philosophy of the poem may find an admirable introduction in the volume of Mr. Da-vies, printed by Messrs. Triibner & Co.

Edwin Arnold, C.S.I.

* "I dare not claim that in more concealed matters I always guess the mind of a poet correctly." fPubJisher's Note]

THE SONG CELESTIAL

CHAPTER I

The Distress of Arjuna

Dhritarashtra. Ranged thus for battle on the sacred plain— On Kurukshetra —say, Sanjaya! say What wrought my people, and the Pandavas?

Sanjaya. When he beheld the host of

Pandavas, Raja Duryodhana to Drona drew, And spake these words: *'Ah, Guru! see this

line, How vast it is of Pandu fighting-men. Embattled by the son of Drupada, Thy scholar in the war! Therein stand ranked Chiefs like Arjuna, like to Bhima chiefs, Benders of bows; Virata, Yuyudhan, Drupada, eminent upon his car, Dhrishtaket, Chekitan, Kasi's stout lord, Purujit, Kuntibhoj, and Saivya, With Yudhamanyu, and Uttamauj, Subhadra's child; and Draupadi's—all

famed!

All mounted on their shining chariots! On our side, too—thou best of Brahmans!

see Excellent chiefs, commanders of my line, Whose names 1 joy to count: thyself the first. Then Bhishma, Karna, Kripa fierce in fight, Vikarna, Aswatthaman; next to these Strong Saumadatti, with full many more Valiant and tried, ready this day to die For me their king, each with his weapon

grasped. Each skillful in the field. Weakest—

meseems— Our battle shows where Bhishma holds

command, And Bhima, fronting him, something too

strong! Have care our captains nigh to Bhishma's

ranks Prepare what help they may! Now, blow my

shell!"

Then, at the signal of the aged king, With blare to wake the blood, rolling around Like to a lion's roar, the trumpeter Blew the great Conch; and, at the noise of it.

Trumpets and drums, cymbals and gongs

and horns Burst into sudden clamor; as the blasts Of loosened tempest, such the tumult

seemed! Then might be seen, upon their car of gold Yoked with white steeds, blowing their

battle-shells, Krishna the God, Arjuna at His side: Krishna, with knotted locks, blew His great

conch Carved of the "Giant's bone"; Arjuna blew India's loud gift; Bhima the terrible— Wolf-bellied Bhima—blew a long reed-conch; And Yudhisthira, Kunti's blameless son. Winded a mighty shell, "Victory's Voice"; And Nakula blew shrill upon his conch Named the "Sweet-sounding," Sahadev on

his Called "Gem-bedecked," and Kasi's Prince

on his. Sikhandi on his car, Dhrishtadyumn, Virata, Satyaki the Unsubdued, Drupada, with his sons (O Lord of Earth!),

Long-armed Subhadra's children, all blew

loud, So that the clangor shook their foemen's

hearts, With quaking earth and thundering heav'n.

Then t'was— Beholding Dhritarashtra's battle set. Weapons unsheathing, bows drawn forth,

the war Instant to break—Arjun, whose ensign-badge Was Hanuman the monkey, spake this thing To Krishna the Divine, his charioteer: "Drive, Dauntless One! to yonder open

ground Betwixt the armies; I would see more nigh These who will fight with us, those we must

slay Today, in war's arbitrament; for, sure, On bloodshed all are bent who throng this

plain, Obeying Dhritarashtra's sinful son."

Thus, by Arjuna prayed (O Bharata!), Between the hosts that heavenly Charioteer Drove the bright car, reining its milk-white steeds

Where Bhishma led, and Drona, and their

Lords. "See!" spake He to Arjuna, "where they

stand, Thy kindred of the Kurus"—and the Prince Marked on each hand the kinsmen of his

house, Grandsires and sires, uncles and brothers

and sons. Cousins and sons-in-law and nephews,

mixed With friends and honored elders; some

this side, Some that side ranged—and, seeing those

opposed, Such kith grown enemies, Arjuna's heart Melted with pity, while he uttered this:

Arjuna. Krishna! as I behold, come here

to shed Their common blood, yon concourse of our

kin. My members fail, my tongue dries in my

mouth, A shudder thrills my body, and my hair Bristles with horror; from my weak hand

slips

Gandiv, the goodly bow; a fever burns My skin to parching; hardly may I stand; The life within me seems to swim and faint; Nothing do I foresee save woe and wail! It is not good, O Keshav! naught of good Can spring from mutual slaughter! Lo, I

hate Triumph and domination, wealth and ease. Thus sadly won! Aho! what victory Can bring delight, Govinda! what rich spoils Could profit; what rule recompense; what

span Of life itself seem sweet, bought with such

blood? Seeing that these stand here, ready to die. For whose sake life was fair, and pleasure

pleased. And power grew precious: grandsires, sires,

and sons, Brothers, and fathers-in-law, and sons-in-law. Elders and friends! Shall 1 deal death on

these Even though they seek to slay us? Not one

blow, O Madhusudan! will I strike to gain

The rule of all Three Worlds; then, how

much less To seize an earthly kingdom! Killing these Must breed but anguish, Krishna! If they be Guilty, we shall grow guilty by their deaths; Their sins will light on us, if we shall slay Those sons of Dhritarashtra, and our kin; What peace could come of that, O Madhava? For if indeed, blinded by lust and wrath. These cannot see, or will not see, the sin Of kingly lines o'erthrown and kinsmen

slain. How should not we, who see, shun such a

crime— We who perceive the guilt and feel the

shame— O Thou Delight of Men, Janardana? By overthrow of houses perisheth Their sweet continuous household piety, And—rites neglected, piety extinct— Enters impiety upon that home;

Its women grow unwomaned, whence there

spring Mad passions, and the mingling-up of castes, Sending a Hell-ward road that family.

And whoso wrought its doom by wicked

wrath. Nay, and the souls of honored ancestors Fall from their place of peace, being bereft Of funeral-cakes and the wan death-water.* So teach our holy hymns. Thus, if we slay Kinsfolk and friends for love of earthly

power, Ahovat! what an evil fault it were! Better I deem it, if my kinsmen strike. To face them weaponless, and bare my breast To shaft and spear, than answer blow with

blow.

So speaking, in the face of those two hosts, Arjuna sank upon his chariot-seat. And let fall bow and arrows, sick at heart.

here endeth chapter i of the Bhagavad-Gita,

Entitled "Arjun-Vishad," Or "The Book of the Distress of Arjuna."

* Some repetitionary lines [verses 43,44] are here omitted.

CHAPTER II

The Book of Doctrines

Sanjaya. Him, filled with such compassion and such grief,

With eyes tear-dimmed, despondent, in stern words

The Driver, Madhusudan, thus addressed:

Krishna. How hath this weakness taken

thee? Whence springs The inglorious trouble, shameful to the

brave. Barring the path of virtue? Nay, Arjun! Forbid thyself to feebleness! it mars Thy warrior-name! cast off the coward-fit! Wake! Be thyself! Arise, Scourge of thy Foes!

Arjuna. How can I, in the battle, shoot with shafts On Bhishma, or on Drona—O Thou Chief!— Both worshipful, both honorable men? 11

Better to live on beggar's bread

With those we love alive, Than taste their blood in rich feasts spread,

And guiltily survive!

Ah! were it worse—who knows?— to be

Victor or vanquished here, When those confront us angrily

Whose death leaves living drear?

In pity lost, by doubtings tossed. My thoughts—distracted—turn

To Thee, the Guide 1 reverence most. That I may counsel learn:

I know not what would heal the grief Burned into soul and sense.

If I were earth's unchallenged chief— A god—and these gone thence!

Sanjaya. So spake Arjuna to the Lord of

Hearts, And sighing, "1 will not fight!" held silence

then. To whom, with tender smile (O Bharata!),

While the Prince wept despairing 'twixt

those hosts, Krishna made answer in divinest verse:

Krishna. Thou grievest where no grief

should be! thou speak'st Words lacking wisdom! for the wise in heart
Mourn not for those that live, nor those that

die. Nor I, nor thou, nor any one of these. Ever was not, nor ever will not
be, Forever and forever afterwards. All that doth live lives always! To man's

frame As there come infancy and youth and age. So come there raisings-up
and layings-down Of other and of other life-abodes. Which the wise know,
and fear not. This

that irks— Thy sense-life, thrilling to the elements— Bringing thee heat
and cold, sorrows and

joys, Tis brief and mutable! Bear with it, Prince! As the wise bear. The soul
which is not

moved. The soul that with a strong and constant calm

Takes sorrow and takes joy indifferently, Lives in the life undying! That
which is Can never cease to be; that which is not Will not exist. To see this

truth of both Is theirs who part essence from accident, Substance from shadow. Indestructible, Learn thou! the Life is, spreading life through

all; It cannot anywhere, by any means, Be anywise diminished, stayed, or changed. But for these fleeting frames which it informs With spirit deathless, endless, infinite. They perish. Let them perish. Prince! and

fight! He who shall say, '*Lo! I have slain a man!" He who shall think, "Lo! I am slain!" those

both Know naught! Life cannot slay. Life is not

slain!

Never the spirit was born; the spirit shall cease to be never; Never was time it was not; End and Beginning are dreams!

Birthless and deathless and changeless remaineth the spirit forever;

Death hath not touched it at all, dead though the house of it seems!

Who knoweth it exhaustless, self-sustained,

Immortal, indestructible—shall such

Say, "1 have killed a man, or caused to kill"?

Nay, but as when one layeth His worn-out robes away,

And, taking new ones, sayeth, "These will I wear today!"

So putteth by the spirit

Lightly its garb of flesh, And passeth to inherit

A residence afresh.

1 say to thee weapons reach not the Life, Flame bums it not, waters cannot o'erwhelm. Nor dry winds wither it. Impenetrable, Unentered, unassailed,

unharmed,

untouched, Immortal, all-arriving, stable, sure. Invisible, ineffable, by word And thought uncompassed, ever all itself— Thus is the Soul declared! How wilt thou,

then—

Knowing it so—grieve when thou shouldst

not grieve? How, if thou hearest that the man new-dead Is, like the man new-born, still living man— One same, existent Spirit—wilt thou weep? The end of birth is death; the end of death Is birth: this is ordained! and mournest thou, Chief of the stalwart arm! for what befalls Which could not otherwise befall? The birth Of living things comes unperceived; the

death Comes unperceived; between them, beings

perceive: What is there sorrowful herein, dear Prince?

Wonderful, wistful, to contemplate! Difficult, doubtful, to speak upon! Strange and great for tongue to relate,

Mystical hearing for everyone! Nor wotteth man this, what a marvel it is, When seeing, and saying, and hearing are done!

This Life within all living things. My Prince!

Hides beyond harm; scorn thou to suffer,

then, For that which cannot suffer. Do thy part! Be mindful of thy name, and tremble not! Naught better can betide a martial soul Than lawful war; happy the warrior To whom comes joy of battle—comes, as

now, Glorious and fair, unsought; opening for him A gateway unto Heav'n. But, if thou shunn'st This honorable field—a Kshatriya— If, knowing thy duty and thy task, thou bidd'st Duty and task go by—that shall be sin! And those to come shall speak thee infamy From age to age; but infamy is worse For men of noble blood to bear than death! The chiefs upon their battle-chariots Will deem 'twas fear that drove thee from

the fray. Of those who held thee mighty-souled the

scorn Thou must abide, while all thine enemies Will scatter bitter speech of thee, to mock The valor which thou hadst—what fate

could fall

More grievously than this? Either—being

killed— Thou wilt win Swarga's safety, or—alive And victor—thou wilt reign an earthly king. Therefore, arise, thou Son of Kunti! brace Thine arm for conflict, nerve thy heart to

meet— As things alike to thee—pleasure or pain, Profit or ruin, victory or defeat: So minded, gird thee to the fight, for so Thou shalt not sin!

Thus far I speak to thee As from the "Sankhya"—unspiritually— Hear now the deeper teaching of the Yog, Which holding, understanding, thou shalt

burst Thy Karmabandh, the bondage of wrought

deeds. Here shall no end be hindered, no hope

marred. No loss be feared: faith—yea, a little faith— Shall save thee from the anguish of thy

dread. Here, Glory of the Kurus! shines one rule— One steadfast rule— while shifting souls

have laws

Many and hard. Specious, but wrongful deem The speech of those ill-taught ones who extol The letter of their Vedas, saying, "This Is all we have, or need"; being weak at heart With wants, seekers of Heaven: which comes

—they say— As "fruit of good deeds done"; promising

men Much profit in new births for works of faith; In various rites abounding; following

whereon Large merit shall accrue towards wealth and

power; Albeit, who wealth and power do most desire Least fixity of soul have such, least hold On heavenly meditation. Much these teach. From Veds, concerning the "three qualities"; But thou, be free of the "three qualities," Free of the "pairs of opposites,"* and free From that sad righteousness which calculates; Self-ruled, Arjuna! simple, satisfiedit Look! like as when a tank pours water forth To suit all needs, so do these Brahmans draw

* Technical phrases of Vedic religion. t The whole of this passage is highly involved and difficult to render.

Text for all wants from tank of Holy VWit. But thou, want not! ask not! Find full reward Of doing right in right! Let right deeds be Thy motive, not the fruit which comes from

them. And live in action! Labor! Make thine acts Thy piety, casting all self aside, Contemning gain and merit; equable In good or evil: equability Is Yog, is piety!

Yet, the right act Is less, far less, than the right-thinking mind. Seek refuge in thy soul; have there thy

heaven! Scorn them that follow virtue for her gifts! The mind of pure devotion—even here— Casts equally aside good deeds and bad, Passing above them. Unto pure devotion Devote thyself: with perfect meditation Comes perfect act, and the right-hearted

rise— More certainly because they seek no gain— Forth from the bands of body, step by step. To highest seats of bliss. When thy firm soul Hath shaken off those tangled oracles

Which ignorantly guide, then shall it soar To high neglect of what's denied or said, This way or that way, in doctrinal writ. Troubled no longer by the priestly lore, Safe shall it live, and sure; steadfastly bent On meditation. This is Yog—and Peace!

Arjuna. What is his mark who hath that

steadfast heart, Confirmed in holy meditation? How Know we his speech, Kesava? Sits he,

moves he Like other men?

Krishna. When one, O Pritha's Son! — Abandoning desires which shake the mind— Finds in his soul full comfort for his soul. He hath attained the Yog —that man is such! In sorrows not dejected, and in joys Not overjoyed; dwelling outside the stress Of passion, fear, and anger; fixed in calms Of lofty contemplation—such an one Is Muni, is the Sage, the true Recluse! He who, to none and nowhere overbound By ties of flesh, takes evil things and good. Neither desponding nor exulting, such

Bears wisdom's plainest mark! He who shall

draw, As the wise tortoise draws its four feet safe Under its shield, his five frail senses back Under the spirit's buckler from the world Which else assails them—such an one, my

Prince! Hath wisdom's mark! Things that solicit

sense Hold off from the self-governed; nay, it

comes. The appetites of him who lives beyond Depart, aroused no more. Yet may it

chance, O Son of Kunti! that a governed mind Shall sometime feel the sense-storms sweep,

and wrest Strong self-control by the roots. Let him

regain His kingdom! let him conquer this, and sit On Me intent. That man alone is wise Who keeps the mastery of himself! If one Ponders on objects of the sense, there springs Attraction; from attraction grows desire; Desire flames to fierce passion; passion

breeds

Recklessness; then the memory—all

betrayed— Lets noble purpose go, and saps the mind, Till purpose, mind, and man are all undone. But, if one deals with objects of the sense. Not loving and not hating, making them Serve his free soul, w^hich rests serenely

lord, Lo! such a man comes to tranquillity; And out of that tranquillity shall rise The end and healing of his earthly pains. Since the will governed sets the soul at

peace. The soul of the ungoverned is not his, Nor hath he knowledge of himself; which

lacked. How grows serenity? and, wanting that. Whence shall he hope for happiness?

The mind That gives itself to follow shows of sense Seeth its helm of wisdom rent away, And, like a ship in waves of whirlwind,

drives To ureck and death. Only with him, great

Prince!

Whose senses are not swayed by things of

sense— Only with him who holds his mastery— Shows wisdom perfect. What is midnight-gloom To unenlightened souls shines wakeful day To his clear gaze; what seems as wakeful

day Is known for night, thick night of ignorance, To his true-seeing eyes. Such is the Saint!

And, like the ocean, day by day receiving Floods from all lands, which never overflows— Its boundary-line not leaping, and not leaving. Fed by the rivers, but unswelled by those—

So is the perfect one! To his soul's

ocean The world of sense pours streams of

witchery; They leave him as they find, without

commotion,

Taking their tribute, but remaining sea.

Yea! whoso, shaking off the yoke of flesh, Lives lord, not servant, of his lusts—set free From pride, from passion, from the sin of

"Self— Toucheth tranquillity! O Pritha's Son! That is the state of Brahm! There rests no

dread When that last step is reached! Live w^here

he will. Die when he may, such passeth from all

'plaining, To blest Nirvana, with the Gods, attaining.

here endeth chapter h of the Bhagavad-Gita,

Entitled "Sankhya-Yog," Or 'The Book of Doctrines."

CHAPTER III

Virtue in Work

Arjuna. Thou whom all mortals praise, Janardana! If meditation be a nobler thing Than action, wherefore then, great Kesava! Dost thou impel me to this dreadful fight? Now am I by Thy doubtful speech disturbed! Tell me one thing, and tell me certainly: By what road shall I find the better end?

Krishna. I told thee, blameless Lord! there

be two paths Shown to this world, two schools of wisdom.

First The Sankhya's, which doth save in way of

works Prescribed by reason; next, the Yog, which

bids Attain by meditation, spiritually: Yet these are one! No man shall 'scape from

act By shunning action; nay, and none shall

come

By mere renouncements unto perfectness. Nay, and no jot of time, at any time. Rests any actionless; his nature's law Compels him, even unwilling, into act; [For thought is act in fancy]. He who sits Suppressing all the instruments of flesh. Yet in his idle heart thinking on them. Plays the inept and guilty hypocrite; But he who, with strong body serving mind. Gives up his mortal powers to worthy work, Not seeking gain, Arjuna! such an one Is honorable. Do thine allotted task! Work is more excellent than idleness; The body's life proceeds not, lacking work. There is a task of holiness to do— Unlike world-binding toil—which bindeth

not The faithful soul; such earthly duty do Free from desire, and thou shalt well perform Thy heavenly purpose. Spake Prajapati— In the beginning, when all men were made, And, with mankind, the sacrifice—"Do this! Work! sacrifice! Increase and multiply With sacrifice! This shall be Kamadhuk, Your 'Cow of Plenty,' giving back her milk Of all abundance. Worship the gods thereby;

The gods shall yield thee grace. Those meats

ye crave The gods will grant to Labor, when it pays Tithes in the altar-flame. But if one eats Fruits of the earth, rendering to kindly Heaven No gift of toil, that thief steals from his

world."

Who eat of food after their sacrifice Are quit of fault, but they that spread a feast All for themselves eat sin and drink of sin. By food the living live; food comes of rain, And rain comes by the pious sacrifice, And sacrifice is paid with tithes of toil; Thus action is of Brahma, who is One, The Only, All-pervading, at all times Present in sacrifice. He that abstains To help the rolling wheels of this great

world. Glutting his idle sense, lives a lost life, Shameful and vain. Existing for himself, Self-concentrated, serving self alone, No part hath he in aught; nothing achieved, Naught wrought or unwrought toucheth

him; no hope

Of help for all the living things of earth Depends from him.* Therefore, thy task

prescribed With spirit unattached gladly perform, Since in performance of plain duty man Mounts to his highest bliss. By works alone Janak and ancient saints reached

blessedness! Moreover, for the upholding of thy kind. Action thou should'st embrace. What the

wise choose The unwise people take; what best men do The multitude will follow. Look on Me, Thou Son of Pritha! in the three wide worlds I am not bound to any toil—no height Awaits to scale, no gift remains to gain— Yet 1 act here! and, if I acted not— Earnest and watchful—those that look to Me For guidance, sinking back to sloth again Because I slumbered, would decline from

good. And I should break earth's order and commit Her offspring unto ruin, Bharata! Even as the unknowing toil, wedded to sense,

* I am doubtful of accuracy here.

So let the enlightened toil, sense-freed, but

set To bring the world deliverance, and its bliss; Not sowing in those simple, busy hearts Seed of despair. Yea! let each play his part In all he finds to do, with unyoked soul. All things are everywhere by Nature virought In interaction of the qualities. The fool, cheated by self, thinks, 'This I did" And "That I v^ought"; but—ah, thou strong-armed Prince! — A better-lessoned mind, knowing the play Of visible things within the world of sense, And how the qualities must qualify, Standeth aloof even from his acts.

Th' untaught Live mixed with them, knowing not Nature's

way. Of highest aims unwitting, slow and dull. Those make thou not to stumble, having the

light; But all thy dues discharging, for My sake. With meditation centered inwardly— Seeking no profit, satisfied, serene. Heedless of issue—fight! They who shall keep

My ordinance thus, the wise and willing

hearts, Have quittance from all issue of their acts; But those who disregard My ordinance. Thinking they know, know naught, and fall

to loss, Confused and foolish. 'Sooth, the instructed

one Doth of his kind, following what fits him

most; And lower creatures of their kind, in vain Contending 'gainst the law. Needs must it be The objects of the sense will stir the sense To like and dislike, yet th' enlightened man Yields not to these, knowing them enemies. Finally, this is better, that one do His own task as he may, even though he fail, Than take tasks not his own, though they

seem good. To die performing duty is no ill; But who seeks other roads shall wander still.

Arjuna. Yet tell me. Teacher! by what force doth man Go to his ill, unwilling—as if one Pushed him that evil path?

Krishna. Kama it is!

Passion it is! born of the Darknesses, Which pusheth him. Mighty of appetite, Sinful, and strong is this!—man's enemy! As smoke blots the white fire, as clinging rust Mars the bright mirror, as the womb

surrounds The babe unborn—so is the world of things Foiled, soiled, enclosed in this desire of

flesh. The wise fall, caught in it; the unresting foe It is of wisdom, wearing countless forms. Fair but deceitful, subtle as a flame. Sense, mind, and reason—these, O Kunti's

Son! Are booty for it; in its play with these It maddens man, beguiling, blinding him. Therefore, thou noblest child of Bharata! Govern thy heart! Constrain th' entangled

sense! Resist the false, soft sinfulness which saps Knowledge and judgment! Yea, the world is

strong, But what discerns it stronger, and the mind Strongest; and high o'er all the ruling Soul.

Wherefore, perceiving Him who reigns

supreme, Put forth full force of Soul in thy own soul! Fight! vanquish foes and doubts, dear Hero!

slay What haunts thee in fond shapes, and would

betray!

here endeth chapter hi of the Bhagavad-Gita,

Entitled "Karma-Yog," Or "The Book of Virtue in Work."

CHAPTER IV

The Religion of Knowledge

Krishna. This deathless Yoga, this deep

union, I taught Vivaswata,* the Lord of Light; Vivaswata to Manu gave it; he To Ikshwaku; so passed it down the line Of all My royal Rishis. Then, with years, The truth grew dim and perished, noble

Prince! Now once again to thee it is declared— This ancient lore, this mystery supreme— Seeing I find thee votary and friend.

Arjuna. Thy birth, dear Lord, was in these

later days. And bright Vivaswata's preceded time! How shall I comprehend this thing thou

sayest, "From the beginning it was 1 who taught?"

Krishna. Manifold the renewals of My birth * A name of the sun.

Have been, Arjuna! and of thy births, too! But Mine I know, and thine thou knowest not,

0 Slayer of thy Foes! Albeit I be Unborn, undying, indestructible.

The Lord of all things living; not the less— By Maya, by My magic which I stamp On floating Nature-forms, the primal vast—

1 come, and go, and come. When

Righteousness Declines, O Bharata! when Wickedness Is strong, I rise, from age to age, and take Visible shape, and move a man with men. Succoring the good, thrusting the evil back, And setting Virtue on her seat again. Who knows the truth touching My births on

earth And My divine work, when he quits the

flesh Puts on its load no more, falls no more down To earthly birth: to Me he comes, dear Prince!

Many there be who come! from fear set free. From anger, from desire; keeping their hearts Fixed upon Me—My Faithful—purified

By sacred flame of Knowledge. Such as these Mix with My being. Whoso worship Me, Them I exalt; but all men everywhere Shall fall into My path; albeit, those souls Which seek reward for works, make sacrifice Now, to the lower gods. I say to thee Here have they their reward. But I am He Made the Four Castes, and portioned them

a place After their qualities and gifts. Yea, I Created, the Reposeful; I that live Immortally, made all those mortal births: For works soil not My essence, being works Wrought uninvolved.* Who knows Me

acting thus Unchained by action, action binds not him; And, so perceiving, all those saints of old Worked, seeking for deliverance. Work thou As, in the days gone by, thy fathers did.

Thou sayst, perplexed—it hath been asked before By singers and by sages —"What is act, And what inaction?" I will teach thee this,

* Without desire of fruit.

And, knowing, thou shalt learn which work

doth save. Needs must one rightly meditate those three: Doing, not doing, and undoing. Here Thorny and dark the path is! He who sees How action may be rest, rest action—he Is wisest 'mid his kind; he hath the truth! He doeth well, acting or resting. Freed In all his works from prickings of desire, Burned clean in act by the white fire of

truth— The wise call that man wise; and such an

one. Renouncing fruit of deeds, always content, Always self-satisfying, if he works. Doth nothing that shall stain his separate

soul. Which—quit of fear and hope, subduing

self. Rejecting outward impulse, yielding up To body's need nothing save body—dwells Sinless amid all sin, with equal calm Taking what may befall, by grief unmoved, Unmoved by joy, unenvyingly; the same In good and evil fortunes; nowise bound By bond of deeds. Nay, but of such an one.

Whose crave is gone, whose soul is liberate, Whose heart is set on truth—of such an one,

What work he does is work of sacrifice, Which passeth purely into ash and smoke Consumed upon the altar! All's then God! The sacrifice is Brahm, the ghee and grain Are Brahm, the fire is Brahm, the flesh it eats

Is Brahm; and unto Brahm attaineth he Who, in such office, meditates on Brahm. Some votaries there be who serve the gods With flesh and altar-smoke; but other some Who, lighting subtler fires, make purer rite With will of worship. Of the which be they Who, in white flame of continence, consume Joys of the sense, delights of eye and ear. Forgoing tender speech and sound of song: And they who, kindling fires with torch of

Truth, Burn on a hidden altar-stone the bliss Of youth and love, renouncing happiness: And they who lay for offering there their

wealth. Their penance, meditation, piety,

Their steadfast reading of the scrolls, their

lore Painfully gained with long austerities: And they who, making silent sacrifice. Draw in their breath to feed the flame of

thought. And breathe it forth to waft the heart on

high. Governing the ventage of each entering air Lest one sigh pass which helpeth not the

soul: And they who, day by day denying needs. Lay life itself upon the altar-flame. Burning the body wan. Lo! all these keep The rite of offering, as if they slew Victims; and all thereby efface much sin. Yea! and who feed on the immortal food Left of such sacrifice, to Brahma pass. To The Unending. But for him that makes No sacrifice, he hath nor part nor lot Even in the present world. How should he share Another, O thou Glory of thy Line?

In sight of Brahma all these offerings Are spread and are accepted! Comprehend

That all proceed by act; for knowing this, Thou shalt be quit of doubt. The sacrifice Which Knowledge pays is better than great

gifts Offered by wealth, since gifts' worth, O My

Prince! Lies in the mind which gives, the will that

serves; And these are gained by reverence, by strong

search, By humble heed of those who see the Truth And teach it. Knowing Truth, thy heart no

more Will ache with error, for the Truth shall show All things subdued to thee, as thou to Me. Moreover, Son of Pandu! wert thou worst Of all wrong-doers, this fair ship of Truth Should bear thee safe and dry across the sea Of thy transgressions. As the kindled flame Feeds on the fuel till it sinks to ash, So unto ash, Arjuna! unto naught The flame of Knowledge wastes works' dross

away! There is no purifier like thereto In all this world, and he who seeketh it

Shall find it—being grown perfect—in

himself. Believing, he receives it when the soul Masters itself, and cleaves to Truth, and

comes— Possessing knowledge—to the higher peace, The uttermost repose. But those untaught. And those without full faith, and those who

fear Are shent; no peace is here or other where— No hope, nor happiness for whoso doubts. He that, being self-contained, hath

vanquished doubt. Disparting self from service, soul from

works, Enlightened and emancipate. My Prince! Works fetter him no more! Cut then atwain With sword of wisdom, Son of Bharata! This doubt that binds thy heart-beats! cleave

the bond Born of thy ignorance! Be bold and wise! Give thyself to the field with Me! Arise! here endeth chapter iv of the Bhagavad-Gita, Entitled "/nana Yog," Or "The Book of the Religion o/KnowJedge."

CHAPTER V

Religion by Renouncing Fruit of Works

Arjuna. Yet, Krishna! at the one time

Thou dost laud Surcease of works, and at another time, Service through work. Of these twain plainly

tell Which is the better way?

Krishna. To cease from works

Is well, and to do works in holiness Is well; and both conduct to bliss supreme; But of these twain the better way is his Who working piously refraineth not.

That is the true Renouncer, firm and fixed. Who—seeking naught, rejecting naught—

dwells proof Against the "opposites."* O valiant Prince! In doing, such breaks lightly from all deed—

* That is "joy and sorrow, success and failure, heat and cold," etc.

Tis the new scholar talks as they were two, This Sankhya and this Yoga—wise men

know Who husbands one plucks golden fruit of

both! The region of high rest which Sankhyans

reach Yogins attain. Who sees these twain as one Sees with clear eyes! Yet such abstraction,

Chief! Is hard to win without much holiness. Whoso is fixed in holiness, self-ruled, Pure-hearted, lord of senses and of self. Lost in the common life of all which lives— A "Yogayukt"—he is a Saint who wends Straightway to Brahm. Such an one is not

touched By taint of deeds. "Naught of myself I do!" Thus will he think, who holds the truth of

truths— In seeing, hearing, touching, smelling; when He eats, or goes, or breathes; slumbers or

talks. Holds fast or loosens, opens his eyes or shuts; Always assured 'This is the sense-world

plays

RELIGION BY RENOUNCING FRUIT OF WORKS 45

With senses." He that acts in thought of

Brahm, Detaching end from act, with act content, The world of sense can no more stain his soul Than waters mar th' enameled lotus-leaf. With life, with heart, with mind—nay,

with the help Of all five senses—letting selfhood go, Yogins toil ever towards their souls' release. Such votaries, renouncing fruit of deeds, Gain endless peace; the unvowed, the

passion-bound, Seeking a fruit from works, are fastened down. The embodied sage, withdrawn within his

soul, At every act sits godlike in "the town Which hath nine gateways,"* neither doing

aught Nor causing any deed. This world's Lord

makes Neither the work, nor passion for the work, Nor lust for fruit of work; the man's own self Pushes to these! The Master of this World Takes on himself the good or evil deeds

* i.e., the body.

Of no man—dwelling beyond! Mankind

errs here By folly, darkening knowledge. But, for

whom That darkness of the soul is chased by light. Splendid and clear shines manifest the Truth As if a Sun of Wisdom sprang to shed Its beams of dawn. Him meditating still. Him seeking, with Him blended, stayed on

Him, The souls illuminated take that road Which hath no turning back— their sins

flung off By strength of faith. [Who will may have this

Light; Who hath it sees.] To him who wisely sees. The Brahman with his scrolls and sanctities. The cow, the elephant, the unclean dog, The Outcast gorging dog's meat, are all one.

The world is overcome—aye! even here! By such as fix their faith on Unity. The sinless Brahma dwells in Unity, And they in Brahma. Be not over-glad Attaining joy, and be not over-sad

RELIGION BY RENOUNCING FRUIT OF WORKS 47

Encountering grief; but stayed on Brahma,

still Constant let each abide! The sage whose

soul Holds off from outer contacts, in himself Finds bliss; to Brahma joined by piety. His spirit tastes eternal peace. The joys Springing from sense-life are but quickening

wombs Which breed sure griefs: those joys begin

and end! The wise mind takes no pleasure, Kunti's

Son! In such as those! But if a man shall learn, Even while he lives and bears his body's

chain, To master lust and anger, he is blest! He is the Yukta; he hath happiness, Contentment, light, within: his life is merged In Brahma's life; he doth Nirvana touch! Thus go the Rishis unto rest, who dwell With sins effaced, with doubts at end, with

hearts Governed and calm. Glad in all good they

live, Nigh to the peace of God; and all those live

Who pass their days exempt from greed and

wrath, Subduing self and senses, knowing the Soul!

The Saint who shuts outside his placid

soul All touch of sense, letting no contact through; Whose quiet eyes gaze straight from fixed

brows, Whose outward breath and inward breath

are drawn Equal and slow through nostrils still and

close; That one—with organs, heart, and mind

constrained, Bent on deliverance, having put away Passion, and fear, and rage—hath, even

now. Obtained deliverance, ever and ever freed. Yea! for he knows Me Who am He that heeds The sacrifice and worship, God revealed; And He who heeds not, being Lord of Worlds, Lover of all that lives, God unrevealed. Wherein who will shall find surety and

shield!

RELIGION BY RENOUNCING FRUIT OF WORKS 49

here ends chapter v of the Bhagavad-Gita,

Entitled "Karmasanyasayog/"

Or 'The Book of Religion by Renouncing

Fruit of Works/'

CHAPTER VI

Religion by Self-Restraint

Krishna. Therefore, who doeth work rightful to do, Not seeking gain from work, that man, O

Prince! Is Sannyasi and Yogi— both in one— And he is neither who lights not the flame Of sacrifice, nor setteth hand to task.

Regard as true Renouncer him that makes Worship by work, for who renounceth not Works not as Yogin. So is that well said: "By works the votary doth rise to saint. And saintship is the ceasing from all works"; Because the perfect Yogin acts—but acts Unmoved by passions and unbound by

deeds, Setting result aside.

Let each man raise The Self by Soul, not trample down his

Self,

[52 . THE SONG CELESTIAL \

Since Soul that is Self's friend may grow

Self's foe. Soul is Self's friend when Self doth rule o'er

Self, But Self turns enemy if Soul's own self Hates Self as not itself.*

The sovereign soul Of him who lives self-governed and at peace Is centered in itself, taking alike Pleasure and pain; heat, cold; glory and

shame. He is the Yogi, he is Yukta, glad With joy of light and truth— dwelling apart Upon a peak, with senses subjugate Whereto the clod, the rock, the glistering

gold Show all as one. By this sign is he known Being of equal grace to comrades, friends. Chance-comers, strangers, lovers, enemies. Aliens and kinsmen—loving all alike, Evil or good.

Sequestered should he sit. Steadfastly meditating, solitary,

* The Sanskrit has this play on the double meaning of Atman.

His thoughts controlled, his passions laid

away, Quit of belongings. In a fair, still spot Having his fixed abode—not too much

raised. Nor yet too low—let him abide, his goods A cloth, a deerskin, and the Kusa-grass. There, setting hard his mind upon The One, Restraining heart and senses, silent, calm, Let him accomplish Yoga, and achieve Pureness of soul, holding immovable Body and neck and head, his gaze absorbed Upon his nose-end,* rapt from all around. Tranquil in spirit, free of fear, intent Upon his Brahmacharya vow, devout. Musing on Me, lost in the thought of Me. That Yogin, so devoted, so controlled. Comes to the peace beyond—My peace, the

peace Of high Nirvana!

But for earthly needs Religion is not his who too much fasts Or too much feasts, nor his who sleeps away An idle mind, nor his who wears to waste

* So in original.

His strength in vigils. Nay, Arjuna! call That the true piety which most removes Earth-aches and ills, where one is moderate In eating and in resting

34

and in sport— Measured in wish and act—sleeping betimes, Waking betimes for duty.

When the man, So living, centers on his soul the thought Straitly restrained —untouched internally By stress of sense—then is he Yukta. See! Steadfast a lamp burns sheltered from the

wind— Such is the likeness of the Yogi's mind Shut from sense-storms and burning bright

to Heaven. When mind broods placid, soothed with

holy wont; When Self contemplates self, and in itself Hath comfort; when it knows the nameless

joy Beyond all scope of sense, revealed to soul. Only to soul! and, knowing, wavers not. True to the farther Truth; when, holding this, It deems no other treasure comparable. But, harbored there, cannot be stirred or

shook

By any gravest grief—call that state "peace," That happy severance Yoga; call that man The perfect Yogin!

Steadfastly the will Must toil thereto, till efforts end in ease, And thought has passed from thinking.

Shaking off All longings bred by dreams of fame and

gain. Shutting the doorways of the senses close With watchful ward; so, step by step, it

comes To gift of peace assured and heart assuaged, When the mind dwells self-wrapped, and the

soul broods Cumberless. But, as often as the heart Breaks—wild and wavering—from control, so oft Let him re-curb it, let him rein it back To the soul's governance; for perfect bliss Grows only in the bosom tranquilized. The spirit passionless, purged from

offence. Vowed to the Infinite. He who thus vows His soul to the Supreme Soul, quitting sin.

Passes unhindered to the endless bliss Of unity with Brahma. He so vowed, So blended, sees the Life-Soul resident In all things living, and all living things In that Life-Soul contained. And whoso thus Discerneth Me in all, and all in Me, I never let him go, nor looseneth he Hold upon Me; but, dwell he where he may, Whate'er his life, in Me he dwells and lives, Because he knows and worships Me, Who

dwell In all which lives, and cleaves to Me in all. Arjuna! if a man sees everywhere— Taught by his own similitude—one Life, One Essence in the Evil and the Good, Hold him a Yogi, yea! well-perfected!

Arjuna. Slayer of Madhu! yet again, this

Yog, This Peace, derived from equanimity, Made known by Thee—I see no fixity Therein, no rest, because the heart of men Is unfixed, Krishna! rash, tumultuous, Willful and strong. It were all one, I think, To hold the wayward wind, as tame man's

heart.

Krishna. Hero long-armed! beyond denial, hard Man's heart is to restrain, and wavering; Yet may it grow restrained by habit, Prince! By wont of self-command. This Yog, I say, Cometh not lightly to th' ungoverned ones; But he who will be master of himself Shall win it, if he stoutly strive thereto.

Arjuna. And what road goeth he who,

having faith. Fails, Krishna! in the striving—falling back From holiness, missing the perfect rule? Is he not lost, straying from Brahma's light. Like the vain cloud, which floats 'twixt earth and heaven When lightning splits it, and it vanisheth? Fain would I hear Thee answer me herein, Since, Krishna! none save Thou can clear

the doubt.

Krishna. He is not lost, thou Son of Pritha!

No! Nor earth, nor heaven is forfeit, even for him. Because no heart that holds one right desire Treadeth the road of loss! He who should

fail.

Desiring righteousness, cometh at death Unto the Region of the Just; dwells there Measureless years, and being born anew, Beginneth life again in some fair home Amid the mild and happy. It may chance He doth descend into a Yogin house On Virtue's breast, but that is rare! Such birth Is hard to be obtained on this earth, Chief! So hath he back again what heights of heart He did achieve, and so he strives anew To perfectness, with better hope, dear Prince! For by the old desire he is drawn on Unwittingly; and only to desire The purity of Yog is to pass Beyond the Sabdabrahm, the spoken Ved. But, being Yogi, striving strong and long, Purged from transgressions, perfected by

births Following on births, he plants his feet at last Upon the farther path. Such an one ranks Above ascetics, higher than the wise. Beyond achievers of vast deeds! Be thou Yogi, Arjuna! And of such believe, Truest and best is he who worships Me With inmost soul, stayed on My Mystery!

I

religion by self-restraint 59

here endeth chapter vi of the Bhagavad-Gita,

Entitled "Atmasanyamayog," Or 'The Book of Religion by Self-Restraint."

CHAPTER VII

Religion by Discernment

Krishna. Learn now, dear Prince! how, if

thy soul be set Ever on Me—still exercising Yog, Still making Me thy Refuge—thou shalt

come Most surely unto perfect hold of Me. I will declare to thee that utmost lore, Whole and particular, which, when thou

knowest, Leaveth no more to know here in this world.

Of many thousand mortals, one,

perchance, Striveth for Truth; and of those few that

strive— Nay, and rise high—one only—here and

there— Knoweth Me, as 1 am, the very Truth.

Earth, water, flame, air, ether, life, and mind,

And individuality—those eight Make up the showing of Me, Manifest.

These be My lower Nature; learn the higher, Whereby, thou Valiant One! this Universe Is, by its principle of life, produced; Whereby the worlds of visible things are

born As from a Yoni. Know! I am that womb— I make and I unmake this Universe— Than Me there is no other Master, Prince! No other Maker! All these hang on Me As hangs a row of pearls upon its string. I am the fresh taste of the water; 1 The silver of the moon, the gold o' the sun. The word of worship in the Veds, the thrill That passeth in the ether, and the strength Of man's shed seed. I am the good sweet

smell Of the moistened earth, 1 am the fire's red

light, The vital air moving in all which moves. The holiness of hallowed souls, the root Undying, whence hath sprung whatever is; The wisdom of the wise, the intellect Of the informed, the greatness of the great.

The splendor of the splendid. Kunti's Son! These am I, free from passion and desire; Yet am 1 right desire in all who yearn, Chief of the Bharatas! for all those moods, Soothfast, or passionate, or ignorant, Which Nature frames, deduce from Me;

but all Are merged in Me—not 1 in them! The

world— Deceived by those three qualities of being— Wotteth not Me Who am outside them all, Above them all. Eternal! Hard it is To pierce that veil divine of various shows Which hideth Me; yet they who worship Me Pierce it and pass beyond.

1 am not known To evil-doers, nor to foolish ones. Nor to the base and churlish; nor to those Whose mind is cheated by the show of things. Nor those that take the way of Asuras.*

Four sorts of mortals know Me: he who weeps, Arjuna! and the man who yearns to know; And he who toils to help; and he who sits

* Beings of low and devilish nature.

Certain of Me, enlightened.

Of these four, O Prince of India! highest, nearest, best That last is, the devout soul, wise, intent Upon "The One." Dear, above all, am 1 To him; and he is dearest unto Me! All four are good, and seek Me; but Mine

ov^n, The true of heart, the faithful—stayed on

Me, Taking Me as their utmost blessedness. They are not "Mine," but 1— even I Myself! At end of many births to Me they come! Yet hard the wise Mahatma is to find. That man who sayeth, "All is Vasudev!"*

There be those, too, whose knowledge,

turned aside By this desire or that, gives them to serve Some lower gods, with various rites,

constrained By that which mouldeth them. Unto all

such— Worship what shrine they will, what shapes,

in faith—

* Krishna.

Tis I who give them faith! I am content! The heart thus asking favor from its God, Darkened but ardent, hath the end it craves, The lesser blessing— but 'tis I v^ho give! Yet soon is withered what small fruit they

reap: Those men of little minds, who worship so. Go where they worship, passing with their

gods. But Mine come unto Me! Blind are the eyes Which deem th' Unmanifested manifest, Not comprehending Me in My true Self! Imperishable, viewless, undeclared. Hidden behind My magic veil of shows, I am not seen by all; I am not known— Unborn and changeless—to the idle world. But I, Arjuna! know all things which were. And all which are, and all which are to be. Albeit not one among them knoweth Me!

By passion for the "pairs of opposites," By those twain snares of Like and Dislike,

Prince! All creatures live bewildered, save some few Who, quit of sins, holy in act, informed,

Freed from the "opposites," and fixed in

faith, Cleave unto Me.

Who cleave, who seek in Me Refuge from birth* and death, those have the

Truth! Those know Me Brahma; know Me Soul of

Souls, The Adhyatman; know Karma, My work; Know I am Adhibhuta, Lord of Life, And Adhidaiva, Lord of all the Gods, And Adhiyajna, Lord of Sacrifice; Worship Me well, with hearts of love and

faith, And find and hold Me in the hour of death.

here endeth chapter vh of the Bhagavad-Gita,

Entitled "Vijnanayog," Or 'The Book of Religion by Discernment."

* I read here janma, "birth"; not/ara, "age."

CHAPTER VIII

Religion by Devotion

to the One Supreme God

Arjuna. Who is that Brahma? What that Soul of Souls, The Adhyatman? What, Thou Best of All! Thy work, the Karma? Tell me what it is Thou namest Adhibhuta? What again Means Adhidaiva? Yea, and how it comes Thou canst be Adhiyajna in Thy flesh? Slayer of Madhu! Further, make me know How good men find Thee in the hour of death?

Krishna. 1 Brahma am! the One Eternal God, And Adhyatman is My Being's name, The Soul of Souls! What goeth forth from Me, Causing all life to live, is Karma called; And, Manifested in divided forms, I am the Adhibhuta, Lord of Lives; And Adhidaiva, Lord of all the Gods, Because 1 am Purusha, Who begets. And Adhiyajna, Lord of Sacrifice,

I—speaking with thee in this body here—

Am, thou embodied one! (for all the shrines

Flame unto Me!) And, at the hour of death.

He that hath meditated Me alone.

In putting off his flesh, comes forth to Me,

Enters into My Being—doubt thou not!

But if he meditated otherwise,

At hour of death, in putting off the flesh.

He goes to what he looked for, Kunti's Son!

Because the Soul is fashioned to its like.

Have Me, then, in thy heart always! and

fight! Thou too, when heart and mind are fixed

on Me, Shalt surely come to Me! All come who

cleave With never-wavering will of firmest faith, Owning none other Gods —all come to Me, The Uttermost, Purusha, Holiest!

Whoso hath known Me, Lord of sage

and singer, Ancient of days; of all the Three

Worlds Stay, Boundless—but unto every atom

Bringer

Of that which quickens it: whoso, I say,

Hath known My form, which passeth mortal knowing; Seen My effulgence —which no eye hath seen— Than the sun's burning gold more brightly glowing, Dispersing darkness—unto him hath been

Right life! And, in the hour when life is ending. With mind set fast and trustful piety. Drawing still breath beneath calm brows unbending, In happy peace that faithful one doth die—

In glad peace passeth to Purusha's heaven. The place which they who read the Vedas name Aksharam, "Ultimate"; whereto have striven

Saints and ascetics—their road is the same.

That way—the highest way—goes he who shuts The gates of all his senses, locks desire Safe in his heart, centers the vital airs Upon his parting thought, steadfastly set; And, murmuring Om, the sacred syllable— Emblem of Brahm —dies, meditating Me.

For who, none other Gods regarding, looks Ever to Me, easily am I gained By such a Yogi; and attaining Me, They fall not—those Mahatmas—back to

birth. To life, which is the place of pain, which

ends. But take the way of utmost blessedness.

The worlds, Arjuna!—even Brahma's world— Roll back again from Death to Life's unrest; But they, O Kunti's Son! that reach to Me, Taste birth no more. If ye know Brahma's Day Which is a thousand Yugas; if ye know The thousand Yugas making Brahma's Night,

Then know ye Day and Night as He doth

know! When that vast Dawn doth break, th' Divisible Is brought anew into the Visible; When that deep Night doth darken, all which

is Fades back again to Him Who sent it forth; Yea! this vast company of living things— Again and yet again produced—expires At Brahma's Nightfall; and at Brahma's

Dawn Riseth, without its will, to life newborn. But—higher, deeper, innermost—abides Another Life, not like the life of sense. Escaping sight, unchanging. This endures When all created things have passed away; This is that Life named the Unmanifest, The Infinite! the All! the Uttermost. Thither arriving none return. That Life Is Mine, and I am there! And, Prince! by faith Which wanders not, there is a way to come Thither. I, the Purusha, I Who spread The Universe around Me—in Whom dwell All living Things—may so be reached and

seen!

Richer than holy fruit on Vedas growing, Greater than gifts, better than prayer or fast,

Such wisdom is! The Yogi, this way knowing Comes to the Utmost Perfect Peace at last.

here endeth chapter vih of the Bhagavad-Gita,

Entitled "Aksharaparabrahmayog," Or 'The Book of Religion by Devotion to the One Supreme God."

* I have discarded ten lines [verses 23-27] of Sanskrit text here as an undoubted interpolation by some Vedantist.

CHAPTER IX

Religion by the Kingly Knowledge and the Kingly Mystery

Krishna. Now will I open unto thee— whose heart

Rejects not—that last lore, deepest-concealed,

That farthest secret of My Heavens and Earths,

Which but to know shall set thee free from ills—

A royal lore! a Kingly mystery!

Yea! for the soul such light as purgeth it

From every sin—a light of holiness

With inmost splendor shining, plain to see,

Easy to walk by, inexhaustible!

They that receive not this, failing in faith To grasp the greater wisdom, reach not Me, Destroyer of thy foes! They sink anew Into the realm of Flesh, where all things change!

By Me the whole vast Universe of things Is spread abroad—by Me, the Unmanifest! In Me are all existences contained; Not I in them!

Yet they are not contained, Those visible things! Receive and strive to

embrace The mystery majestical! My Being— Creating all, sustaining all— still dwells Outside of all!

See! as the shoreless airs Move in the measureless space, but are not

space [And space were space without the moving

airs]; So all things are in Me, but are not I.

At closing of each Kalpa, Indian Prince! All things which be back to My Being come; At the beginning of each Kalpa, all Issue new-born from Me.

By Energy And help of Prakriti, My outer Self,

Again, and yet again, I make go forth The realms of visible things—without their

will— All of them—by the power of Prakriti.

Yet these great makings. Prince! involve

Me not, Enchain Me not! 1 sit apart from them. Other, and Higher, and Free —nowise

attached!

Thus doth the stuff of worlds, moulded by Me, Bring forth all that which is, moving or still. Living or lifeless! Thus the worlds go on!

The minds untaught mistake Me, veiled

in form— Naught see they of My secret Presence,

naught Of My hid Nature, ruling all which lives. Vain hopes pursuing, vain deeds doing; fed On vainest knowledge, senselessly they seek An evil way, the way of brutes and fiends. But My Mahatmas, those of noble soul Who tread the path celestial, worship Me

With hearts unwandering—knowing Me

the Source, Th' Eternal Source, of Life. Unendingly They glorify Me; seek Me; keep their vows Of reverence and love, with changeless faith Adoring Me. Yea, and those too adore. Who, offering sacrifice of wakened hearts. Have sense of one pervading Spirit's stress— One Force in every place, though manifold! I am the Sacrifice! I am the Prayer! I am the Funeral-Cake set for the dead! I am the healing herb! I am the ghee. The Mantra, and the flame, and that which

burns! I am—of all this boundless Universe— The Father, Mother, Ancestor, and Guard! The end of Learning! That which purifies In lustral water! I am Om! I am Rig-Veda, Sama Veda, Yajur-Ved; The Way, the Fosterer, the Lord, the Judge, The Witness; the Abode, the Refuge-House, The Friend, the Fountain and the Sea of Life Which sends, and swallows up; Treasure of

Worlds And Treasure-Chamber! Seed and Seed-Sower,

Whence endless harvests spring! Sun's heat

is mine; Heaven's rain is Mine to grant or to withhold; Death am I, and Immortal Life I am, Arjuna! Sat and Asat, Visible Life, And Life Invisible!

Yea! those who learn The threefold Veds, who drink the Soma-wine, Purge sins, pay sacrifice—from Me they earn Passage to Swarga, where the meats divine

Of great gods feed them in high Indra's heaven. Yet they, when that prodigious joy is o'er. Paradise spent, and wage for merits given. Come to the world of death and change once more

They had their recompense! they stored their treasure,

Following the threefold Scripture

and its writ; Who seeketh such gaineth the fleeting

pleasure Of joy which comes and goes!

I grant them it!

But to those blessed ones who worship Me, Turning not otherwise, with minds set fast, I bring assurance of full bliss beyond.

Nay, and of hearts which follow other gods In simple faith, their prayers arise to Me, O Kunti's Son! though they pray

wrongfully; For I am the Receiver and the Lord Of every sacrifice, which these know not Rightfully; so they fall to earth again! Who follow gods go to their gods; who vow Their souls to Pitris go to Pitris; minds To evil Bhuts given o'er sink to the Bhuts; And whoso loveth Me cometh to Me. Whoso shall offer Me in faith and love A leaf, a flower, a fruit, water poured forth. That offering I accept, lovingly made With pious will. Whate'er thou doest. Prince!—

Eating or sacrificing, giving gifts, Praying or fasting—let it all be done For Me, as Mine. So shalt thou free thyself FromKarmabandh, the chain which holdeth

men To good and evil issue: so shalt come Safe unto Me—when thou art quit of flesh— By faith and abdication joined to Me!

1 am alike for all! I know not hate, 1 know not favor! What is made is Mine! But them that worship Me with love, I love; They are in Me, and I in them!

Nay, Prince! If one of evil life turn in his thought Straightly to Me, count him amidst the

good; He hath the high way chosen; he shall grow Righteous ere long; he shall attain that peace Which changes not. Thou Prince of India! Be certain none can perish, trusting Me! O Pritha's Son! whoso will turn to Me, Though they be born from the very womb

of Sin, Woman or man, sprung of the Vaisya caste Or lowly disregarded Sudra—all

Plant foot upon the highest path—how then The holy Brahmans and My Royal Saints? Ah! ye who into this ill world are come— Fleeting and false —set your faith fast on Me! Fix heart and thought on Me! Adore Me!

Bring Offerings to Me! Make Me prostrations!

Make Me your supremest joy! and, undivided, Unto My rest your spirits shall be guided.

here endeth chapter ix of the Bhagavad-Gita,

Entitled "Rajavidyarajaguhyayog,"

Or 'The Book of Religion by the KingJy

Knowledge and the KingJy Mystery."

CHAPTER X

Religion by the Heavenly Perfections

Krishna.* Hear farther yet, thou Long-Armed Lord! these latest words I say — Uttered to bring thee bhss and peace, who lovest Me alway—

Not the great company of gods nor kingly

Rishis know My Nature, Who have made the gods and

Rishis long ago;

He only knoweth—only he is free of sin, and

wise, Who seeth Me, Lord of the Worlds, with

faith-enlightened eyes.

Unborn, undying, unbegun. Whatever Natures be

* The Sanskrit poem here rises to an elevation of style and manner which I
have endeavored to mark by change of meter.

To mortal men distributed, those natures spring from Me!

Intellect, skill, enlightenment, endurance,

self-control, Truthfulness, equability, and grief or joy

of soul.

And birth and death, and fearfulness, and

fearlessness, and shame, And honor, and sweet harmlessness,* and

peace which is the same

Whate'er befalls, and mirth, and tears, and

piety, and thrift. And wish to give, and will to help—all

Cometh of My gift!

The Seven Chief Saints, the Elders Four, the

Lordly Manus set— Sharing My work—to rule the worlds, these

too did I beget;

And Rishis, Pitris, Manus, all, by one thought

of My mind; Thence did arise, to fill this world, the races

of mankind;

* Ahimsa.

Wherefrom who comprehends My Reign of

mystic Majesty— That truth of truths—is thenceforth linked

in faultless faith to Me:

Yea! knowing Me the source of all, by Me

all creatures wrought, The wise in spirit cleave to Me, into My

Being brought;

Hearts fixed on Me; breaths breathed to Me;

praising Me, each to each, So have they happiness and peace, with

pious thought and speech;

And unto these—thus serving well, thus

loving ceaselessly— I give a mind of perfect mood, whereby they

draw to Me;

And all for love of them, within their

darkened souls 1 dwell. And with bright rays of wisdom's lamp,

their ignorance dispel.

Arjuna. Yes! Thou art Parabrahm! The High Abode! The Great Purification! Thou art God

Eternal, All-creating, Holy, First, Without beginning! Lord of Lords and Gods! Declared by all the Saints—by Narada, Vyasa, Asita, and Devalas— And here Thyself declaring unto me! What Thou hast said now know I to be truth, O Kesava! that neither gods nor men Nor demons comprehend Thy mystery Made manifest, Divinest! Thou Thyself Thyself alone dost know, Maker Supreme! Master of all the living! Lord of Gods! King of the Universe! To Thee alone Belongs to tell the heavenly excellence Of those perfections wherewith Thou dost

fill These worlds of Thine—Pervading,

Immanent! How shall I learn, Supremest Mystery! To know Thee, though I muse continually? Under what form of Thine unnumbered

forms Mayest Thou be grasped? Ah! yet again

recount. Clear and complete. Thy great appearances. The secrets of Thy Majesty and Might, Thou High Delight of Men! Never enough

Can mine ears drink the Amrit* of such words!

Krishna. Hantal So be it! Kuru Prince! I will to thee unfold Some portions of My Majesty, whose powers are manifold!

I am the Spirit seated deep in every creature's

heart; From Me they come; by Me they live; at My

word they depart!

Vishnu of the Adityas I am, those Lords of

Light; Maritchi of the Maruts, the Kings of Storm

and Blight;

By day I gleam, the golden Sun of burning

cloudless Noon; By Night, amid the asterisms 1 glide, the

dappled Moon!

Of Vedas I am Sama-Ved, of gods in India's

Heaven Vasava; of the faculties to living beings given

The mind which apprehends and thinks; of

Rudras Sankara; * The nectar of Immortality.

Of Yakshas and of Rakshasas, Vittesh; and Pavaka

Of Vasus, and of mountain-peaks Meru;

Vrihaspati Know Me 'mid planetary Powers; 'mid

Warriors heavenly

Skanda; of all the water-floods the Sea which

drinketh each, And Bhrigu of the holy Saints, and Om of

sacred speech;

Of prayers the prayer ye whisper;* of hills

Himala's snow, And Aswattha, the fig-tree, of all the trees

that grow;

Of the Devarshis, Narada; and Chitrarath

of them That sing in Heaven, and Kapila of Munis,

and the gem

Of flying steeds, Uchchaisravas, from Amrit-

wave which burst; Of elephants Airavata; of males the Best and

First;

* Called "The Jap."

Of weapons Heav'n's hot thunderbolt; of

cows white Kamadhuk, From whose great milky udder-teats all

heart's desires are strook;

Vasuki of the serpent-tribes, round Mandara

entwined; And thousand-fanged Ananta, on whose

broad coils reclined

Leans Vishnu; and of water-things Varuna;

Aryam Of Pitris, and of those that judge, Yama the

Judge I am;

Of Daityas dread Prahlada; of what metes

days and years. Time's self I am; of woodland-beasts—

buffaloes, deers, and bears—

The lordly-painted tiger; of birds the vast

Garud, The whirlwind 'mid the winds; 'mid chiefs

Rama with blood imbrued,

Makar 'mid fishes of the sea, and Ganges

'mid the streams; Yea! First, and Last, and Center of all which

is or seems

I am, Arjuna! Wisdom Supreme of what is

wise, Words on the uttering hps I am, and eyesight

of the eyes.

And "A" of written characters, Dwandwa*

of knitted speech, And Endless Life, and boundless Love,

whose power sustaineth each;

And bitter Death which seizes all, and

joyous sudden Birth, Which brings to light all beings that are to be

on earth;

And of the viewless virtues. Fame, Fortune,

Song am I, And Memory, and Patience; and Craft, and

Constancy:

Of Vedic hymns the Vrihatsam, of meters

Gayatri, Of months the Margasirsha, of all the seasons

three

The flower-wreathed Spring; in dicer's-play the conquering Double-Eight;

* The compound form of Sanskrit words.

The splendor of the splendid, and the greatness of the great,

Victory I am, and Action! and the goodness

of the good. And Vasudev of Vrishni's race, and of this

Pandu brood

Thyself!—Yea, My Arjuna! thyself; for thou

art Mine! Of poets Usana, of saints Vyasa, sage divine;

The policy of conquerors, the potency of

kings, The great unbroken silence in learning's

secret things; The lore of all the learned, the seed of all

which springs.

Living or lifeless, still or stirred, v^hatever

beings be. None of them is in all the worlds, but it

exists by Me!

Nor tongue can tell, Arjuna! nor end of telling

come Of these My boundless glories, whereof I

teach thee some;

For wheresoe'er is wondrous work, and

majesty, and might. From Me hath all proceeded. Receive thou

this aright!

Yet how shouldst thou receive, O Prince!

the vastness of this word? I, who am all, and made it all, abide its

separate Lord!

here endeth chapter x of the Bhagavad-Gita,

Entitled "Vibhuti Yog,"

Or 'The Book of Religion by the Heavenly

Perfections."

CHAPTER XI

The Manifesting of the One and Manifold

Arjuna. This, for my soul's peace, have I

heard from Thee, The unfolding of the Mystery Supreme Named Adhyatman—comprehending

which, My darkness is dispelled; for now I know, O Lotus-eyed!* whence is the birth of men, And whence their death, and what the

majesties Of Thine immortal rule. Fain would 1 see, As Thou Thyself declar'st it. Sovereign Lord! The likeness of that glory of Thy Form Wholly revealed. O Thou Divinest One! If this can be, if I may bear the sight. Make Thyself visible. Lord of all prayers! Show me Thy very self, the Eternal God!

Krishna. Gaze then, thou Son of Pritha! I manifest for thee

* "Kamalapatraksha."

Those hundred thousand thousand shapes that clothe My Mystery:

I show thee all My semblances—infinite,

rich, divine— My changeful hues, My countless forms.

See! in this face of Mine,

Adityas, Vasus, Rudras, As wins, and

Maruts; see Wonders unnumbered, Indian Prince!

revealed to none save thee.

Behold! this is the Universe!—Look! what is

live and dead I gather all in one—in Me! Gaze, as thy lips

have said.

On God Eternal, Very God! See Me! see what thou prayest!

Thou canst not!—nor, with human eyes, Arjuna! ever mayest!

Therefore 1 give thee sense divine. Have

other eyes, new light! And, look! This is My glory, unveiled to

mortal sight!

Sanjaya. Then, O King! the God, so saying. Stood, to Pritha's Son displaying

All the splendor, wonder, dread Of His vast Almighty-head.

Out of countless eyes beholding, Out of countless mouths commanding,

Countless mystic forms enfolding In one Form; supremely standing,

Countless radiant glories wearing, Countless heavenly weapons bearing,

Crowned with garlands of star-clusters, Robed in garb of woven lusters.

Breathing from His perfect Presence Breaths of every subtle essence

Of all heavenly odors; shedding Blinding brilliance; overspreading—

Boundless, beautiful—all spaces With His all-regarding faces—

So He showed! If there should rise Suddenly within the skies

Sunburst of a thousand suns

Flooding earth with beams undeemed-of, Then might be that Holy One's

Majesty and radiance dreamed of!

So did Pandu's Son behold All this universe enfold

All its huge diversity

Into one vast shape, and be

Visible, and viewed, and blended In one Body—subtle, splendid.

Nameless—th' All-comprehending God of Gods, the Never-Ending Deity!

But, sore amazed. Thrilled, o'erfilled, dazzled, and dazed,

Arjuna knelt, and bowed his head, And clasped his palms and cried, and said:

Arjuna. Yea! I have seen! I see! Lord! all is wrapped in Thee!

The gods are in Thy glorious frame! the creatures Of earth, and heaven, and hell In Thy Divine form dwell; And in Thy countenance shine all the features

Of Brahma, sitting lone

Upon His lotus-throne; Of saints and sages, and the serpent races

Ananta, Vasuki;

Yea! mightiest Lord! I see Thy thousand thousand arms, and breasts, and faces,

And eyes—on every side Perfect, diversified— And nowhere end of Thee, nowhere beginning. Nowhere a center! Shifts— Wherever soul's gaze lifts — Thy central Self, all-wielding, and all-winning!

Infinite King! I see The anadem on Thee,

The club, the shell, the discus; see Thee burning In beams insufferable. Lighting earth, heaven, and hell With brilliance blinding, glowing, flashing —turning

Darkness to dazzling day.

Look I whichever way. Ah, Lord! I worship Thee—the Undivided,

The Uttermost of thought.

The Treasure-Palace wrought To hold the wealth of the worlds, the Shield provided

To shelter Virtue's laws.

The Fount whence Life's stream draws All waters of all rivers of all being;

The One Unborn, Unending,

Unchanging and Unblending! With might and majesty, past thought, past seeing!

Silver of moon and gold Of sun are glories rolled From Thy great eyes— Thy visage, beaming tender

Throughout the stars and skies, Doth to warm life surprise Thy Universe. The worlds are filled with wonder

Of Thy perfections! Space Star-sprinkled, and void place

From pole to pole of the Blue, from bound to bound. Hath Thee in every spot— Thee, Thee! Where Thou art not,

O Holy, Marvelous Form! is nowhere found!

O Mystic, Awful One! At sight of Thee, made known. The Three Worlds quake; the lower gods draw nigh Thee, They fold their palms, and bow Body, and breast, and brow. And, whispering worship, laud and magnify Thee!

Rishis and Siddhas cry "Hail! Highest Majesty!" From sage and singer breaks the hymn of glory

In dulcet harmony, Sounding the praise of Thee; While countless companies take up the story—

Rudras, who ride the storms,

Th' Adityas' shining forms, Vasus and Sadhyas, Viswas, Ushmapas;

Maruts, and those great Twins,

The heavenly, fair As wins, Gandharvas, Rakshasas, Siddhas, and Asuras*
—

These see Thee, and revere In sudden-stricken fear; Yea! the Worlds—
seeing Thee with form stupendous. With faces manifold, With eyes which
all behold. Unnumbered eyes, vast arms, members tremendous,

Flanks, lit with sun and star. Feet planted near and far,

* These are all divine or deified orders of the Hindu Pantheon.

Tushes of terror, mouths wrathful and tender— The Three wide Worlds
before Thee Adore, as I adore Thee, Quake, as I quake, to witness so much
splendor!

I mark Thee strike the skies With front in wondrous wise Huge, rainbow-
painted, glittering; and Thy mouth Opened, and orbs which see All things,
whatever be In all Thy worlds, east, west, and north and south.

O Eyes of God! O Head!

My strength of soul is fled; Gone is heart's force, rebuked is mind's desire!

When I behold Thee so.

With awful brows a-glow. With burning glance, and lips lighted by fire,

Fierce as those flames which shall Consume, at close of all,

Earth, Heaven! Ah me! I see no Earth and Heaven!

Thee, Lord of Lords! I see,

Thee only—only Thee! Nov^ let Thy mercy unto me be given,

Thou Refuge of the World! Lo! to the cavern hurled Of Thy wide-opened
throat, and lips white-tushed, I see our noblest ones, Great Dhritarashtra's

sons, Bhishma, Drona, and Kama, caught and crushed!

The Kings and Chiefs drawn in,

That gaping gorge within; The best of both these armies torn and riven!

Between Thy jaws they lie

Mangled full bloodily. Ground into dust and death! Like streams down-driven

With helpless haste, which go In headlong furious flow

Straight to the gulfing deeps of th' unfilled ocean, So to that flaming cave Those heroes great and brave Pour, in unending streams, vi^ith helpless motion!

Like moths vy^hich in the night

Flutter towards a light. Drawn to their fiery doom, flying and dying.

So to their death still throng,

Blind, dazzled, borne along Ceaselessly, all those multitudes, wild flying!

Thou, that hast fashioned men,

Devourest them again. One with another, great and small, alike!

The creatures whom Thou mak'st.

With flaming jaws Thou tak'st. Lapping them up! Lord God! Thy terrors strike

From end to end of earth, Filling life full, from birth To death, with deadly, burning, lurid dead!

Ah, Vishnu! make me know Why is Thy visage so? Who art Thou, feasting thus upon Thy dead!

Who? awful Deity!

I bow myself to Thee, Namostu Te, Devavara! Prasid!*

O Mightiest Lord! rehearse

Why hast Thou face so fierce? Whence doth this aspect horrible proceed?

Krishna. Thou seest Me as Time who kills. Time who brings all to doom,
The Slayer Time, Ancient of Days, come hither to consume;

Excepting thee, of all these hosts of hostile

chiefs arrayed. There stands not one shall leave alive the

battlefield! Dismayed No longer be! Arise! obtain renown!

destroy thy foes! Fight for the kingdom waiting thee when

thou hast vanquished those. By Me they fall—not thee! the stroke of

death is dealt them now, * "Hail to Thee, God of Gods! Be favorable!"

Even as they show thus gallantly; My instrument art thou!

Strike, strong-armed Prince, at Drona! at

Bhishma strike! deal death On Karna, Jayadratha; stay all their warlike

breath!

Tis I who bid them perish! Thou wilt but

slay the slain; Fight! they must fall, and thou must live,

victor upon this plain!

Sanjaya. Hearing mighty Keshav's word, Tremblingly that helmed Lord

Clasped his lifted palms, and—praying Grace of Krishna—stood there, saying,

With bowed brow and accents broken. These words, timorously spoken:

Arjuna. Worthily, Lord of Might!

The whole world hath delight In Thy surpassing power, obeying Thee;

The Rakshasas, in dread

At sight of Thee, are sped To all four quarters; and the company

Of Siddhas sound Thy name. How should they not proclaim

Thy Majesties, Divinest, Mightiest?

Thou Brahm, than Brahma greater!

Thou Infinite Creator! Thou God of gods, Life's Dwelling-place and Rest!

Thou, of all souls the Soul! The Comprehending Whole! Of Being formed, and formless Being the Framer; O Utmost One! O Lord! Older than eld. Who stored The worlds with wealth of life! O Treasure-Claimer,

Who wottest all, and art

Wisdom Thyself! O Part In all, and All; for all from Thee have risen!

Numberless now I see

The aspects are of Thee! Vayu* Thou art, and He who keeps the prison

Of Narak, Yama dark; And Agni's shining spark; Varuna's waves are Thy waves. Moon and starlight

* The wind.

Are Thine! Prajapati Art Thou, and 'tis to Thee They knelt in worshiping the old world's far light,

The first of mortal men.

Again, Thou God! again A thousand thousand times be magnified!

Honor and worship be—

Glory and praise—to Thee Namo, Namaste, cried on every side;

Cried here, above, below.

Uttered when Thou dost go, Uttered where Thou dost come! Namol we call;

Namostul God adored!

Namostul Nameless Lord! Hail to Thee! Praise to Thee! Thou One in all;

For Thou art All! Yea, Thou! Ah! if in anger now Thou shouldst remember I did think Thee Friend, Speaking with easy speech. As men use each to each; Did call Thee "Krishna," "Prince," nor comprehend

Thy hidden majesty,

The might, the awe of Thee; Did, in my heedlessness, or in my love.

On journey, or in jest.

Or when we lay at rest, Sitting at council, straying in the grove,

Alone, or in the throng.

Do Thee, most Holy! wrong. Be Thy grace granted for that witless sin!

For Thou art, now I know,

Father of all below. Of all above, of all the worlds within,

Guru of Gurus, more

To reverence and adore Than all which is adorable and high!

How, in the wide worlds three

Should any equal be? Should any other share Thy Majesty?

Therefore, with body bent And reverent intent, I praise, and serve, and seek Thee, asking grace.

As father to a son, As friend to friend, as one Who loveth to his lover, turn Thy face

In gentleness on me!

Good is it I did see This unknown marvel of Thy Form! But fear

Mingles v^ith joy! Retake,

Dear Lord! for pity's sake Thine earthly shape, v^hich earthly eyes may bear!

Be merciful, and shov^

The visage that I know^; Let me regard Thee, as of yore, arrayed

With disc and forehead-gem.

With mace and anadem, Thou that sustainest all things! Undismayed

Let me once more behold

The form I loved of old, Thou of the thousand arms and countless eyes!

This frightened heart is fain

To see restored again My Charioteer, in Krishna's kind disguise.

Krishna. Yea! thou hast seen, Arjuna! because I loved thee well, The secret countenance of Me, revealed by mystic spell.

Shining, and wonderful, and vast, majestic,

manifold. Which none save thou in all the years had

favor to behold;

For not by Vedas cometh this, nor sacrifice,

nor alms, Nor works well-done, nor penance long, nor

prayers, nor chanted psalms.

That mortal eyes should bear to view the

Immortal Soul unclad. Prince of the Kurus! This was kept for thee

alone! Be glad!

Let no more trouble shake thy heart because

thine eyes have seen My terror with My glory. As 1 before have

been

So will I be again for thee; with lightened

heart behold! Once more I am thy Krishna, the form thou

knew'st of old!

Sanjaya. These words to Arjuna spake Vasudev, and straight did take

Back again the semblance dear Of the well-loved charioteer;

Peace and joy it did restore

When the Prince beheld once more

Mighty Brahma's form and face Clothed in Krishna's gentle grace.

Arjuna. Now that I see come back,

Janardana! This friendly human frame, my mind can

think Calm thoughts once more; my heart beats

still again!

Krishna. Yea! it was wonderful and

terrible To view me as thou didst, dear Prince! The

Gods Dread and desire continually to view! Yet not by Vedas, nor from sacrifice. Nor penance, nor gift-giving, nor with prayer Shall any so behold, as thou hast seen! Only by fullest service, perfect faith,

And uttermost surrender am I known And seen, and entered into, Indian Prince! Who doeth all for Me; who findeth Me In all; adoreth always; loveth all Which I have made, and Me, for Love's sole

end, That man, Arjuna! unto Me doth wend.

here endeth chapter xi of the Bhagavad-Gita,

Entitled "Viswarupadarsanam,"

Or 'The Book of the Manifesting of the One

and Manifold."

The Religion of Faith

Arjuna. Lord! of the men who serve

Thee—true in heart— As God revealed; and of the men who serve, Worshiping Thee Unrevealed, Unbodied,

Far, Which take the better way of faith and life?

Krishna. Whoever serve Me—as I show

Myself— Constantly true, in full devotion fixed. Those hold I very holy. But who serve, Worshiping Me, The One, The Invisible, The Unrevealed, Unnamed, Unthinkable, Uttermost, All-pervading, Highest, Sure— Who thus adore Me, mastering their senses. Of one set mind to all, glad in all good. These blessed souls come unto Me.

Yet, hard The travail is for such as bend their minds To reach th' Unmanifest. That viewless path Shall scarce be trod by man bearing the

flesh!

Ill

But whereso any doeth all his deeds Renouncing self for Me, full of Me, fixed To serve only the Highest, night and day Musing on Me—him will I swiftly lift Forth from life's ocean of distress and death Whose soul clings fast to Me. Cling thou to

Me! Clasp Me with heart and mind! so shalt thou

dwell Surely with Me on high. But if thy thought Droops from such height; if thou be'st weak

to set Body and soul upon Me constantly. Despair not! give Me lower service! seek To reach Me, worshiping with steadfast will; And, if thou canst not worship steadfastly. Work for Me, toil in works pleasing to Me! For he that laboreth right for love of Me Shall finally attain! But, if in this Thy faint heart fails, bring Me thy failure!

find Refuge in Me! let fruits of labor go, Renouncing hope for Me, with lowliest

heart. So shalt thou come; for, though to know is

more

Than diligence, yet worship better is Than knowing, and renouncing better still. Near to renunciation—very near— Dwelleth Eternal Peace!

Who hateth naught Of all which lives, living himself benign, Compassionate, from arrogance exempt, Exempt from love of self, unchangeable By good or ill; patient, contented, firm In faith, mastering himself, true to his word, Seeking Me, heart and soul; vowed unto

Me— That man I love! Who troubleth not his kind, And is not troubled by them; clear of v^ath. Living too high for gladness, grief, or fear, That man I love! Who, dwelling quiet-eyed,* Stainless, serene, well-balanced,

unperplexed. Working with Me, yet from all works

detached, That man 1 love! Who, fixed in faith on Me, Dotes upon none, scorns none; rejoices not. And grieves not, letting good or evil hap Light when it will, and when it will depart,

* "Not peering about," anapeksha.

That man I love! Who, unto friend and foe Keeping an equal heart, with equal mind Bears shame and glory; with an equal peace Takes heat and cold, pleasure and pain;

abides Quit of desires, hears praise or calumny In passionless restraint, unmoved by each, Linked by no ties to earth, steadfast in Me, That man 1 love! But most of all I love Those happy ones to whom 'tis life to live In single fervid faith and love unseeing. Drinking the blessed Amrit of my Being!

here endeth chapter xh of the Bhagavad-Gita,

Entitled "Bhaktiyogr Or "The Book of the Religion of Faith.*'

CHAPTER XIII

Religion by Separation of Matter and Spirit

Arjuna. Now would I hear, O gracious Kesava!* Of Life which seems, and Soul beyond, which

sees. And what it is we know—or think to know.

Krishna. Yea! Son of Kunti! for this flesh

ye see Is Kshetra, is the field where Life disports; And that which views and knows it is the

Soul, Kshetrajna. In all "fields," thou Indian

prince! I am Kshetrajna. I am what surveys! Only that knowledge knows which knows

the known By the knower! What it is, that "field" of

life, What qualities it hath, and whence it is,

* The Calcutta edition of the Mahabharata has these three opening lines.
115

And why it changeth, and the facuUy That wotteth it, the mightiness of this, And how it wotteth—hear these things from Me!

The elements, the conscious life, the

mind. The unseen vital force, the nine strange

gates Of the body, and the five domains of sense; Desire, dislike, pleasure and pain, and

thought Deep-woven, and persistency of being; These all are wrought on Matter by the Soul!

Humbleness, truthfulness, and

harmlessness. Patience and honor, reverence for the wise. Purity, constancy, control of self. Contempt of sense-delights, self-sacrifice. Perception of the certitude of ill In birth, death, age, disease, suffering, and

sin;

* I omit two lines of the Sanskrit here, evidently interpolated by some Vedantist.

Detachment, lightly holding unto home, Children, and wife, and all that bindeth

men; An ever-tranquil heart in fortunes good And fortunes evil, w^ith a will set firm To worship Me—Me only! ceasing not; Loving all solitudes, and shunning noise Of foolish crowds; endeavors resolute To reach perception of the Utmost Soul, And grace to understand what gain it were So to attain —this is true Wisdom, Prince! And what is otherwise is ignorance!

Now will I speak of knowledge best to

know— That Truth which giveth man Amrit to drink. The Truth of Him, the Para-Brahm, the All, The Uncreated; not Asat, not Sat, Not Form, nor the Unformed; yet both, and

more— Whose hands are everywhere, and

everywhere Planted His feet, and everywhere His eyes Beholding, and His ears in every place Hearing, and all His faces everywhere Enlightening and encompassing His worlds.

Glorified in the senses He hath given, Yet beyond sense He is; sustaining all, Yet dwells He unattached: of forms and

modes Master, yet neither form nor mode hath He; He is within all beings— and without— Motionless, yet still moving; not discerned For subtlety of instant presence; close To all, to each, yet measurelessly far! Not manifold, and yet subsisting still In all which lives; forever to be known As the Sustainer, yet, at the End of Times, He maketh all to end—and re-creates. The Light of Lights He is, in the heart of the

Dark Shining eternally. Wisdom He is And Wisdom's way, and Guide of all the

wise. Planted in every heart.

So have 1 told Of Life's stuff, and the moulding, and the

lore To comprehend. Whoso, adoring Me, Perceiveth this, shall surely come to Me!

Know thou that Nature and the Spirit both

Have no beginning! Know that qualities And changes of them are by Nature wrought; That Nature puts to work the acting frame, But Spirit doth inform it, and so cause Feeling of pain and pleasure. Spirit, linked To moulded matter, entereth into bond With qualities by Nature framed, and, thus Married to matter, breeds the birth again In good or evil yonis.*

Yet is this— Yea! in its bodily prison!—Spirit pure, Spirit supreme; surveying, governing. Guarding, possessing; Lord and Master still PuRUSHA, Ultimate, One Soul with Me.

Whoso thus knows himself, and knows

his soul PuRUSHA, working through the qualities With Nature's modes, the light hath come

for him! Whatever flesh he bears, never again Shall he take on its load. Some few there be By meditation find the Soul in Self Self-schooled; and some by long philosophy And holy life reach thither; some by works.

* Wombs.

Some, never so attaining, hear of light From other lips, and seize, and cleave to it Worshiping; yea! and those—to teaching

true— Overpass Death!

Wherever, Indian Prince! Life is—of moving things, or things unmoved. Plant or still seed—know^, w^hat is there hath

grown By bond of Matter and of Spirit: Know He sees indeed who sees in all alike The living, lordly Soul; the Soul Supreme, Imperishable amid the Perishing: For, whoso thus beholds, in every place, In every form, the same, one. Living Lord, Doth no more wrongfulness unto himself, But goes the highest road which brings to

bliss. Seeing, he sees, indeed, who sees that works Are Nature's wont, for Soul to practice by Acting, yet not the agent; sees the mass Of separate living things—each of its kind— Issue from One, and blend again to One: Then hath he Brahma, he attains!

O Prince! That Ultimate, High Spirit, Uncreate, Unqualified, even when it entereth flesh Taketh no stain of acts, worketh in naught! Like to th' ethereal air, pervading all. Which, for sheer subtlety, avoideth taint. The subtle Soul sits everyv^here, unstained: Like to the light of the all-piercing sun [Which is not changed by aught it shines

upon] The Soul's light shineth pure in every place; And they who, by such eye of wisdom, see How Matter, and what deals with it, divide; And how the Spirit and the flesh have strife, Those wise ones go the way which leads to

Life!

here endeth chapter xhi of the Bhagavad-Gita,

Entitled "Kshetrakshetrajnavibhagayog,"

Or "The Book of Religion by Separation of

Matter and Spirit."

CHAPTER XIV

Religion by Separation from the Qualities

Krishna. Yet farther will 1 open unto thee This wisdom of all wisdoms, uttermost, The which possessing, all My saints have

passed To perfectness. On such high verities Reliant, rising into fellowship With Me, they are not born again at birth Of KaJpas, nor at PraJayas suffer change!

This Universe the Womb is where I plant Seed of all lives! Thence, Prince of India,

comes Birth to all beings! Whoso, Kunti's Son! Mothers each mortal form, Brahma conceives. And I am He that fathers, sending seed!

SattwQ, Rajas, and Tamas —so are named The qualities of Nature —"Soothfastness," "Passion," and "Ignorance." These three bind down

The changeless Spirit in the changeful

flesh. Whereof sweet "Soothfastness," by purity Living unsullied and enlightened, binds The sinless Soul to happiness and truth; And Passion, being kin to appetite And breeding impulse and propensity, Binds the embodied Soul, O Kunti's Son! By tie of works. But Ignorance, begot Of Darkness, blinding mortal men, binds

down Their souls to stupor, sloth, and drowsiness. Yea, Prince of India! Soothfastness binds

souls In pleasant wise to flesh; and Passion binds By toilsome strain; but Ignorance, which

blots The beams of wisdom, binds the soul to

sloth. Passion and Ignorance, once overcome. Leave Soothfastness, O Bharata! Where this With Ignorance are absent. Passion rules; And Ignorance in hearts not good nor quick. When at all gateways of the Body shines The Lamp of Knowledge, then may one see

well

Soothfastness settled in that city reigns; Where longing is, and ardor, and unrest, Impulse to strive and gain, and avarice, Those spring from Passion —Prince! —

engrained; and w^here Darkness and dullness, sloth and stupor

are, 'Tis Ignorance hath caused them, Kuru

Chief!

Moreover, when a soul departeth, fixed In Soothfastness, it goeth to the place— Perfect and pure—of those that know all

Truth. If it departeth in set habitude Of Impulse, it shall pass into the world Of spirits tied to works; and, if it dies In hardened Ignorance, that blinded soul Is born anew in some unlighted womb.

The fruit of Soothfastness is true and

sweet; The fruit of lusts is pain and toil; the fruit Of Ignorance is deeper darkness. Yea! For Light brings light, and Passion ache to

have. And gloom, bewilderments, and ignorance

Grow forth from Ignorance. Those of the first Rise ever higher; those of the second mode Take a mid place; the darkened souls sink

back To lower deeps, loaded with witlessness!

When, watching life, the living man

perceives The only actors are the Qualities, And knows what rules beyond the Qualities, Then is he come nigh unto Me!

The Soul, Thus passing forth from the Three

Qualities— Whereby arise all bodies—overcomes Birth, Death, Sorrow, and Age; and drinketh deep The undying wine of Amrit.

Arjuna. Oh! my Lord!

Which be the signs to know him that hath

gone Past the Three Modes? How liveth he?

What way Leadeth him safe beyond the threefold

Modes?

Krishna. He who with equanimity

surveys Luster of goodness, strife of passion, sloth Of ignorance, not angry if they are. Not wishful when they are not: he who sits A sojourner and stranger in their midst Unruffled, standing off, saying—serene— When troubles break, 'These be the

Qualities!" He unto whom—Self-centered—grief and

joy Sound as one word; to whose deep-seeing

eyes The clod, the marble, and the gold are one; Whose equal heart holds the same gentleness For lovely and unlovely things, firm-set, Wfell-pleased in praise and dispraise;

satisfied With honor or dishonor; unto friends And unto foes alike in tolerance. Detached from undertakings—he is named Surmounter of the Qualities!

And such— With single, fervent faith adoring Me, Passing beyond the Qualities, conforms

To Brahma, and attains Me!

For I am That whereof Brahma is the likeness! Mine The Amrit is; and Immortality Is mine; and mine perfect Felicity!

HERE ENDETH CHAPTER XIV OF THE Bh AGAV AD-GlTA,

Entitled "Gunatrayavihhagayog,"

Or 'The Book of Religion by Separation

from the Qualities."

CHAPTER XV

Religion by Attaining the Supreme

Krishna. Men call the Aswattha—the

Banyan-tree— Which hath its boughs beneath, its roots

above— The ever-holy tree. Yea! for its leaves Are green and weaving hymns v^hich w^hisper

Truth! Who knows the Asv^attha, knows Veds, and

all.

Its branches shoot to heaven and sink to

earth.* Even as the deeds of men, which take their

birth From qualities: its silver sprays and

blooms,

* I do not consider the Sanskrit verses here— which are somewhat freely rendered—"an attack on the authority of the Vedas," with Mr. Davies, but a beautiful lyrical episode, a new "Parable of the fig tree."

And all the eager verdure of its girth,

Leap to quick life at kiss of sun and air, As men's lives quicken to the temptings fair Of wooing sense: its hanging rootlets seek The soil beneath, helping to hold it there,

As actions wrought amid this world of men

Bind them by ever-tightening bonds again.

If ye knew well the teaching of the Tree,

What its shape saith; and whence it springs;

and,then

How it must end, and all the ills of it. The axe of sharp Detachment ye would whet, And cleave the clinging snaky roots, and lay This Aswattha of sense-life low—to set

New growths upspringing to that happier

sky— Which they who reach shall have no day to

die, Nor fade away, nor fall—to Him, I mean. Father and First, Who made the mystery

Of old Creation; for to Him come they From passion and from dreams who break

away; Who part the bonds constraining them

to flesh, And—Him, the Highest, worshiping alway—

No longer grow at mercy of what breeze Of summer pleasure stirs the sleeping trees. What blast of tempest tears them, bough and stem. To the eternal world pass such as these!

Another Sun gleams there! another Moon! Another Light—not Dusk, nor Dawn, nor

Noon— Which they who once behold return no

more; They have attained My rest, life's Utmost

boon!

When, in this world of manifested life, The undying Spirit, setting forth from Me, Taketh on form, it draweth to itself From Being's storehouse— which containeth all—

Senses and intellect. The Sovereign Soul Thus entering the flesh, or quitting it, Gathers these up, as the wind gathers scents, Blowing above the flower-beds. Ear and Eye, And Touch and Taste, and Smelling, these

it takes— Yea, and a sentient mind—linking itself To sense-things so.

The unenlightened ones Mark not that Spirit when he goes or comes. Nor when he takes his pleasure in the form. Conjoined with qualities; but those see plain Who have the eyes to see. Holy souls see Which strive thereto. Enlightened,

they perceive That Spirit in themselves; but foolish ones. Even though they strive, discern not, having

hearts Unkindled, ill—informed!

Know, too, from Me Shineth the gathered glory of the suns Which lighten all the world: from Me the

moons Draw silvery beams, and fire fierce

loveliness.

I penetrate the clay, and lend all shapes Their living force; I glide into the plant— Root, leaf, and bloom—to make the woodlands green With springing sap. Becoming vital vi^armth, I glow in glad, respiring frames, and pass With outward and with inward breath to

feed The body by all meats.*

For in this world Being is twofold: the Divided, one; The Undivided, one. All things that live Are "the Divided." That which sits apart, 'The Undivided."

Higher still is He, The Highest, holding all, whose Name is

Lord, The Eternal, Sovereign, First! Who fills all

worlds. Sustaining them. And—dwelling thus

beyond Divided Being and Undivided—I Am called of men and Vedas, Life Supreme,

The PURUSHOTTAMA.

* I omit a verse here, evidently interpolated.

Who knows Me thus, With mind unclouded, knoweth all, dear

Prince! And with his whole soul ever worshipeth

Me.

Now is the sacred, secret Mystery Declared to thee! Who comprehendeth this j Hath wisdom! He is quit of works in bliss!

here endeth chapter xv of the Bhagavad-Gita,

Entitled 'Turushottamapraptiyog,"

Or 'The Book of Religion by attaining

the Supreme."

CHAPTER XVI

The Separateness of the Divine and Undivine

Krishna. Fearlessness, singleness of soul,

the will Always to strive for wisdom; opened hand And governed appetites; and piety And love of lonely study; humbleness. Uprightness, heed to injure naught which

lives. Truthfulness, slowness unto wrath, a mind That lightly letteth go what others prize; And equanimity, and charity Which spieth no man's faults; and tenderness Towards all that suffer; a contented heart. Fluttered by no desires; a bearing mild, Modest, and grave, with manhood

nobly mixed, With patience, fortitude, and purity; An unrevengeful spirit, never given To rate itself too high—such be the signs, O Indian Prince! of him whose feet are set On that fair path which leads to heavenly

birth!

Deceitfulness, and arrogance, and pride, Quickness to anger, harsh and evil speech. And ignorance, to its own darkness bhnd— These be the signs, My Prince! of him whose

birth Is fated for the regions of the vile.*

The Heavenly Birth brings to deliverance. So should'st thou know! The birth with

Asuras Brings into bondage. Be thou joyous. Prince! Whose lot is set apart for heavenly Birth.

Two stamps there are marked on all living men. Divine and Undivine; I spake to thee By what marks thou shouldst know the

Heavenly Man, Hear from me now of the Unheavenly!

They comprehend not, the Unheavenly, How Souls go forth from Me; nor how they

come Back unto Me: nor is there Truth in these, Nor purity, or rule of Life. "This world

* "Of the Asuras," Ut.

Hath not a Law, nor Order, nor a Lord," So say they: "Nor hath risen up by Cause Following on Cause, in perfect purposing, But is none other than a House of Lust." And, this thing thinking, all those ruined

ones— Of little wit, dark-minded—give themselves To evil deeds, the curses of their kind. Surrendered to desires insatiable, Full of deceitfulness, folly, and pride. In blindness cleaving to their errors, caught Into the sinful course, they trust this lie As it were true—this lie which leads to

death— Finding in Pleasure all the good which is, And crying "Here it finisheth!"

Ensnared In nooses of a hundred idle hopes. Slaves to their passion and their wrath, they

buy Wealth with base deeds, to glut hot

appetites; "Thus much, today," they say, '*we gained!

thereby Such and such wish of heart shall have its

fill;

And this is ours! and th' other shall be ours! Today we slew a foe, and we will slay Our other enemy tomorrow! Look! Are we not lords? Make we not goodly cheer? Is not our fortune famous, brave, and great? Rich are we, proudly born! What other men Live like to us? Kill, then, for sacrifice! Cast largesse, and be merry!" So they speak Darkened by ignorance; and so they fall— Tossed to and fro with projects, tricked, and

bound In net of black delusion, lost in lusts— Down to foul Naraka. Conceited, fond, Stubborn and proud, dead-drunken with

wine Of wealth, and reckless, all their offerings Have but a show of reverence, being not

made In piety of ancient faith. Thus vowed To self-hood, force, insolence, feasting, wrath, These My blasphemers, in the forms they

wear And in the forms they breed, my foemen are, Hateful and hating; cruel, evil, vile, Lowest and least of men, whom I cast down

Again, and yet again, at end of lives.

Into some devilish w^omb, whence—birth

by birth— The devilish wombs re-spawn them, all

beguiled; And, till they find and worship Me, sweet

Prince! Tread they that Nether Road.

The Doors of Hell Are threefold, whereby men to ruin pass— The door of Lust, the door of VWath, the door Of Avarice. Let a man shun those three! He who shall turn aside from entering All those three gates of Narak, wendeth

straight To find his peace, and comes to Swarga's

gate.

here endeth chapter xvi of the Bhagavad-Gita,

Entitled "Daivasarasaupadwibhagayog,"

Or 'The Book of the Separateness of the

Divine and Undivine."

* I omit the ten concluding slokas, with Mr.

Davies.

CHAPTER XVII

Religion by the Threefold Kinds of Faith

Arjuna. If men forsake the holy ordinance, Heedless of Shastras, yet keep faith at heart And worship, what shall be the state of those, Great Krishna! Sattwan, Rajas, Tamas? Say!

Krishna. Threefold the faith is of mankind, and springs

From those three qualities—becoming "true,"

Or "passion-stained," or "dark," as thou shalt hear!

The faith of each believer, Indian Prince! Conforms itself to what he truly is. Where thou shalt see a worshiper, that one To what he worships lives assimilate: [Such as the shrine, so is the votary], The 'soothfast" souls adore true gods; the souls

Obeying Rajas worship Rakshasas* Or Yakshas; and the men of Darkness pray To Pretas and to Bhutas.t Yea, and those Who practice bitter penance, not enjoined By rightful rule—penance which hath its

root In self-sufficient, proud hypocrisies— Those men, passion-beset, violent, wild. Torturing—the witless ones—My elements Shut in fair company within their flesh, (Nay, Me myself, present within the flesh!) Know them to devils devoted, not to

Heaven! For like as foods are threefold for mankind In nourishing, so is there threefold way Of worship, abstinence, and almsgiving! Hear this of Me! there is a food which brings Force, substance, strength, and health, and

joy to live. Being well-seasoned, cordial, comforting. The "Soothfast" meat. And there be foods

which bring

* Rakshasas and Yakshas are unembodied but capricious beings of great power, gifts, and beauty, sometimes also of benignity.

+ These are spirits of evil, wandering ghosts.

Aches and unrests, and burning blood, and grief.

Being too biting, heating, salt, and sharp,

And therefore craved by too strong appetite.

And there is foul food—kept from overnight,*

Savorless, filthy, which the foul will eat,

A feast of rottenness, meet for the lips

Of such as love the "Darkness."

Thus with rites— A sacrifice not for rewardment made. Offered in rightful wise, when he who vows Sayeth, with heart devout, 'This 1 should

do!" Is "Soothfast" rite. But sacrifice for gain. Offered for good repute, be sure that this, O Best of Bharatas! is Rajas-rite, With stamp of "passion." And a sacrifice Offered against the laws, with no due dole Of food-giving, with no accompaniment Of hallowed hymn, nor largesse to the

priests,

* Yatayaman, food which has remained after the watches of the night. In India this would probably "go bad."

In faithless celebration, call it vile, The deed of "Darkness!"—lost!

Worship of gods Meriting worship; lowly reverence Of Twice-borns, Teachers, Elders; Purity, Rectitude, and the Brahmacharya's vow, And not to injure any helpless thing— These make a true religiousness of Act.

Words causing no man woe, words ever true, Gentle and pleasing words, and those ye say In murmured reading of Sacred VWit— These maketh true religiousness of Speech.

Serenity of soul, benignity, Sway of the silent Spirit, constant stress To sanctify the Nature—these things make Good rite, and true religiousness of Mind.

Such threefold faith, in highest piety Kept, with no hope of gain, by hearts devote Is perfect work of Sattwan, true belief.

Religion shown in act of proud display To win good entertainment, worship, fame,

Such—say I—is of Rajas, rash and vain.

Religion followed by a witless will To torture self, or come at power to hurt Another—'tis of Tamas, dark and ill.

The gift lovingly given, when one shall say "Now must 1 gladly give!" when he who

takes Can render nothing back; made in due place, Due time, and to a meet recipient. Is gift of Sattwan, fair and profitable.

The gift selfishly given, where to receive Is hoped again, or when some end is sought, Or where the gift is proffered with a grudge, This is oiRajas, stained with impulse, ill.

The gift churlishly flung, at evil time, In wrongful place, to base recipient, Made in disdain or harsh unkindliness. Is gift of Tamas, dark; it doth not bless!*

* I omit the concluding sJokas, as of very doubtful authenticity.

here endeth chapter xvii of the Bhagavad-Gita,

Entitled "Sraddhatrayavihhagayog/'

Or 'The Book of Religion by the Threefold

Kinds of Faith."

CHAPTER XVIII

Religion by

Deliverance and Renunciation

Arjuna. Fain would I better know, Thou Glorious One! The very truth—
Heart's Lord!—of Sannyas, Abstention; and Renunciation, Lord! Tyaga;
and what separates these twain!

Krishna. The poets rightly teach that Sannyas Is the forgoing of all acts
which spring Out of desire; and their wisest say Tyaga is renouncing fruit of
acts.

There be among the saints some who have

held All action sinful, and to be renounced; And some who answer, "Nay!
the goodly

acts— As worship, penance, alms—must be

performed!" Hear now My sentence, Best of Bharatas!

Tis well set forth, O Chaser of thy Foes! Renunciation is of threefold form,
And Worship, Penance, Alms, not to be

stayed; Nay, to be gladly done; for all those three Are purifying waters for
true souls!

Yet must be practiced even those high

works In yielding up attachment, and all fruit Produced by works. This is
My judgment,

Prince! This My insuperable and fixed decree!

Abstaining from a work by right

prescribed Never is meet! So to abstain doth spring From "darkness," and
Delusion teacheth it. Abstaining from a work grievous to flesh, When one
saith "Tis unpleasing!" this is

null! Such an one acts from "passion"; naught of

gain Wins his Renunciation! But, Arjun! Abstaining from attachment to the work. Abstaining from rewardment in the work.

While yet one doeth it full faithfully, Saying, " 'Tis right to do!" that is "true" act And abstinence! Who doeth duties so, Unvexed if his work fail, if it succeed Unflattered, in his own heart justified, Quit of debates and doubts, his is "true" act: For, being in the body, none may stand Wholly aloof from act; yet, who abstains From profit of his acts is abstinent.

The fruit of labors, in the lives to come. Is threefold for all men—Desirable, And Undesirable, and mixed of both; But no fruit is at all where no work was.

Hear from me. Long-armed Lord! the makings five Which go to every act, in Sankhya taught As necessary. First the force; and then The agent; next, the various instruments; Fourth, the especial effort; fifth, the God. What work soever any mortal doth Of body, mind, or speech, evil or good. By these five doth he that. Which being thus, Whoso, for lack of knowledge, seeth himself As the sole actor, knoweth naught at all And seeth naught. Therefore, I say, if one—

Holding aloof from self—with unstained

mind Should slay all yonder host, being bid to

slay, He doth not slay; he is not bound thereby!

Knowledge, the thing known, and the

mind which knows, These make the threefold starting-ground of

act. The act, the actor, and the instrument. These make the threefold total of the deed. But knowledge, agent, act, are differenced By three dividing qualities. Hear now Which be the qualities dividing them.

There is "true" Knowledge. Learn thou

it is this: To see one changeless Life in all the Lives, And in the Separate, One Inseparable. There is imperfect Knowledge: that which sees The separate existences apart. And, being separated, holds them real. There is false Knowledge: that which blindly

clings

To one as if 'twere all, seeking no Cause, Deprived of light, narrow, and dull, and "dark."

There is "right" Action: that which—

being enjoined— Is wrought without attachment,

passionlessly, For duty, not for love, nor hate, nor gain. There is "vain" Action: that which men

pursue Aching to satisfy desires, impelled By sense of self, with all-absorbing stress: This is of Rajas —passionate and vain. There is "dark" Action: when one doth a

thing Heedless of issues, heedless of the hurt Or wrong for others, heedless if he harm His own soul—'tis of Tamas, black and bad!

There is the "rightful" doer. He who acts Free from self-seeking, humble, resolute. Steadfast, in good or evil hap the same. Content to do aright—he "truly" acts. There is th' "impassioned" doer. He that works

From impulse, seeking profit, rude and bold To overcome, unchastened; slave by turns Of sorrow and of joy: of Rajas he! And there be evil doers; loose of heart, Low-minded, stubborn, fraudulent, remiss. Dull, slow, despondent—children of the "dark."

Hear, too, of Intellect and Steadfastness The threefold separation, Conqueror-Prince! How these are set apart by Qualities.

Good is the Intellect which comprehends The coming forth and going back of life, What must be done, and what must not be

done. What should be feared, and what should not

be feared, What binds and what emancipates the soul: That is of Sattwan, Prince! of

"soothfastness." Marred is the Intellect which, knowing right And knowing wrong, and what is well to do And what must not be done, yet understands Naught with firm mind, nor as the calm

truth is:

This is oiRajas, Prince! and "passionate!" Evil is Intellect which, wrapped in gloom, Looks upon wrong as right, and sees all

things Contrariwise of Truth. O Pritha's Son! That is of Tamas, "dark" and desperate!

Good is the steadfastness whereby a man Masters his beats of heart, his very breath Of life, the action of his senses; fixed In never-shaken faith and piety: That is of Sattwan, Prince! "soothfast" and

fair! Stained is the steadfastness whereby a man Holds to his duty, purpose, effort, end. For life's sake, and the love of goods to gain, Arjuna! 'tis of Rajas, passion-stamped! Sad is the steadfastness wherewith the fool Cleaves to his sloth, his sorrow, and his fears, His folly and despair. This— Pritha's Son! — Is born of Tamas, "dark" and miserable!

Hear further. Chief of Bharatas! from Me The threefold kinds of Pleasure which there be.

Good Pleasure is the pleasure that

endures, Banishing pain for aye; bitter at first As poison to the soul, but afterward Sweet as the taste of Amrit. Drink of that! It springeth in the Spirit's deep content. And painful Pleasure springeth from the

bond Between the senses and the sense-world.

Sweet As Amrit is its first taste, but its last Bitter as poison. Tis oi Rajas, Prince! And foul and "dark" the pleasure is which springs From sloth and sin and foolishness; at first And at the last, and all the way of life The soul bewildering. Tis of Tamas, Prince!

For nothing lives on earth, nor 'midst the

gods In utmost heaven, but hath its being bound With these three Qualities, by Nature

framed.

The work of Brahmans, Kshatriyas, Vaisyas, And Sudras, O thou Slayer of thy Foes!

Is fixed by reason of the Qualities Planted in each:

A Brahman's virtues, Prince! Born of his nature, are serenity. Self-mastery, religion, purity, Patience, uprightness, learning, and to know The truth of things which be. A Kshatriya's

pride. Born of his nature, lives in valor, fire. Constancy, skillfulness, spirit in fight. And open-handedness and noble mien, As a lord of men. A Vaisya's task, Born with his nature, is to till the ground, Tend cattle, venture trade. A Sudra's state, Suiting his nature, is to minister.

Whoso performeth—diligent, content— The work allotted him, whate'er it be. Lays hold of perfectness! Hear how a man Findeth perfection, being so content: He findeth it through worship—wrought by

work— Of Him that is the Source of all which lives. Of Him by Whom the universe was stretched.

Better thine own work is, though done

with fauh, Than doing others' work, ev'n excellently. He shall not fall in sin who fronts the task Set him by Nature's hand! Let no man leave His natural duty. Prince! though it bear

blame! For every work hath blame, as every flame Is wrapped in smoke! Only that man attains Perfect surcease of work whose work was wrought With mind unfettered, soul wholly subdued. Desires forever dead, results renounced.

Learn from me. Son of Kunti! also this, How one, attaining perfect peace, attains Bblahm, the supreme, the highest height of all!

Devoted—with a heart grown pure, restrained In lordly self-control, forgoing wiles Of song and senses, freed from love and hate, Dwelling 'mid solitudes, in diet spare. With body, speech, and will tamed to obey.

Ever to holy meditation vowed, From passions liberate, quit of the Self, Of arrogance, impatience, anger, pride; Freed from surroundings, quiet, lacking

naught— Such an one groves to oneness with the

Brahm; Such an one, growing one with Brahm,

serene. Sorrows no more, desires no more; his soul, Equally loving all that lives, loves well Me, Who have made them, and attains to Me. By this same love and worship doth he know Me as 1 am, how high and wonderful. And knowing, straightway enters into Me. And whatsoever deeds he doeth— fixed In Me, as in his refuge—he hath won Forever and forever by My grace Th' Eternal Rest! So win thou! In thy

thoughts, Do all thou dost for Me! Renounce for Me! Sacrifice heart and mind and will to Me! Live in the faith of Me! In faith of Me All dangers thou shalt vanquish, by My

grace; But, trusting to thyself and heeding not,

Thou can'st but perish! If this day thou

say'st, Relying on thyself, "I will not fight!" Vain will the purpose prove! thy qualities Would spur thee to the war. What thou dost

shun, Misled by fair illusions, thou wouldst seek Against thy will, when the task comes to thee Waking the promptings in thy nature set. There lives a Master in the hearts of men Maketh their deeds, by subtle pulling-strings. Dance to what tune He will. With all thy soul Trust Him, and take Him for thy succor.

Prince! So—only so, Arjuna!—shalt thou gain— By grace of Him—the uttermost repose, The Eternal Place!

Thus hath been opened thee This Truth of Truths, the Mystery more hid Than any secret mystery. Meditate! And—as thou wilt—then act!

Nay! but once more Take My last word. My utmost meaning have!

Precious thou art to Me; right well-beloved! Listen! I tell thee for thy comfort this. Give Me thy heart! adore Me! serve Me! cling In faith and love and reverence to Me! So shalt thou come to Me! I promise true, For thou art sw^eet to Me

And let go those— Rites and writ duties! Fly to Me alone! Make Me thy single refuge! I will free Thy soul from all its sins! Be of good cheer!

[Hide, the holy Krishna saith. This from him that hath no faith.

Him that worships not, nor seeks Wisdom's teaching when she speaks:

Hide it from all men who mock; But, wherever, 'mid the flock

Of My lovers, one shall teach This divinest, wisest, speech—

Teaching in the faith to bring Truth to them, and offering

Of all honor unto Me— Unto Brahma cometh he!

Nay, and nowhere shall ye find

Any man of all mankind

Doing dearer deed for Me; Nor shall any dearer be

In My earth. Yea, furthermore, Whoso reads this converse o'er,

Held by Us upon the plain, Pondering piously and fain.

He hath paid Me sacrifice! (Krishna speaketh in this wise!)

Yea, and whoso, full of faith, Heareth wisely what it saith,

Heareth meekly—when he dies, Surely shall his spirit rise

To those regions where the Blest, Free of flesh, in joyance rest.]

Hath this been heard by thee, O Indian

Prince! With mind intent? hath all the ignorance— Which bred thy trouble —vanished, My

Arjun?

Arjuna. Trouble and ignorance are gone! the Light Hath come unto me, by Thy favor, Lord!

Now am I fixed! my doubt is fled away! According to Thy word, so will I do!

Sanjaya. Thus gathered I the gracious speech of Krishna, O my King! Thus have I told, with heart a-thrill, this wise and wondrous thing

By great Vyasa's learning writ, how Krishna's

self made known The Yoga, being Yoga's Lord. So is the high

truth shown!

And aye, when I remember, O Lord my King,

again Arjuna and the God in talk, and all this holy

strain,

Great is my gladness: when 1 muse that

splendor, passing speech. Of Hari, visible and plain, there is no tongue

to reach

My marvel and my love and bliss. O Archer-Prince! all hail!

O Krishna, Lord of Yoga! surely there shall not fail

Blessing, and victory, and power, for Thy most mighty sake,

Where this song comes of Arjun, and how with God he spake.

HERE ENDS, WITH CHAPTER XVIII,

Entitled ^'Mokshasanyasayog/'

Or 'The Book of Religion by Deliverance

and Renunciation,"

The Bhagavad-Gita.